Living Lord, Empowering Spirit, Testifying People

Living Lord, Empowering Spirit, Testifying People

The Story of the Church
in the Book of Acts

MEL STORM

WIPF & STOCK · Eugene, Oregon

LIVING LORD, EMPOWERING SPIRIT, TESTIFYING PEOPLE
The Story of the Church in the Book of Acts

Copyright © 2014 Mel Storm. All rights reserved. Except for brief quotations in critical publications or reviews, no part of this book may be reproduced in any manner without prior written permission from the publisher. Write: Permissions. Wipf and Stock Publishers, 199 W. 8th Ave., Suite 3, Eugene, OR 97401.

Wipf & Stock
An Imprint of Wipf and Stock Publishers
199 W. 8th Ave., Suite 3
Eugene, OR 97401

www.wipfandstock.com

ISBN 13: 978-1-62564-407-7

Manufactured in the U.S.A.   12/31/2014

Scripture quotations, unless otherwise indicated, are from the New Revised Standard Version Bible, copyright 1989, Division of Christian Education of the National Council of the Churches of Christ in the United States of America. Used by permission. All rights reserved.

Acts is about the church, and I dedicate this book to the people of my home church, Heritage Church of Christ. My wife, Diane, and I with our four sons have been members of this church for nearly thirty years. This loving community of believers has immeasurably blessed our lives, and this little book is a small expression of my love and appreciation for them.

"And now I commend you to God and to the message of his grace, a message that is able to build you up and to give you the inheritance among all who are sanctified"

—ACTS 20:32

Contents

Acknowledgments | xi
Preface | ix
Abbreviations | xiii

Introduction to the Acts of the Apostles | 1
Acts 1: The Preparation for the Coming of the Holy Spirit | 14

The Church in Jerusalem: Acts 2:1—8:3

Acts 2: The Coming of the Holy Spirit and the Birth of the Church | 25
Acts 3: The Healing of the Lame Man | 35
Acts 4: The First Arrest of Peter and John | 41
Acts 5: Ananias and Sapphira | 48
Acts 6: The Selection of the Seven to Care for Widows | 53
Acts 7:1—8:3: The Speech of Stephen | 58

The First Persecution and Expansion of the Church: Acts 8:4—12:25

Acts 8:4-40: The Ministry of Philip | 65
Acts 9: The Conversion of Saul of Tarsus | 74
Acts 10:1—11:18: The Conversion of Cornelius | 80
Acts 11:19—12:25: The Antioch Church/The Persecution of Herod Agrippa | 88

CONTENTS

The Missionary Journeys of Paul: Acts 13:1—21:17

Acts 13–14: Paul's First Missionary Journey | 99
Acts 15:1–35: The Jerusalem Conference | 109
Acts 15:36—17:15: Paul's Second Missionary Journey:
    Troas, Philippi, Thessalonica, and Berea | 114
Acts 17:16—18:22: Paul's Second Missionary Journey:
    Athens and Corinth | 123
Acts 18:23—19:41: Paul's Third Missionary Journey: Ephesus | 131
Acts 20:1—21:16: Paul's Third Missionary Journey:
    Macedonia, Greece, and Return | 139

The Arrest and Imprisonment of Paul: Acts 21:18—28:31

Acts 21:17—23:11: The Arrest and Imprisonment of
    Paul in Jerusalem | 147
Acts 23:12—26:32: The Imprisonment of Paul in Caesarea | 153
Acts 27–28: Paul's Voyage to Rome | 162

Selected Bibliography | 173

Preface

It is widely understood that Acts is about the church, from its beginning to its numerical growth and geographical expansion over a period of about thirty years. In my church tradition, this book has had a profound influence in the shaping of faith and practice. In fact, I have reserved some space to address certain topics of interpretation of Acts that have been of particular interest in my tradition. Nevertheless, my intention is to show how Acts speaks to disciples of Jesus from all traditions.

Acknowledgments

This book is the result of many years of teaching the Book of Acts to undergraduate students. I wanted to provide my students a book to supplement their reading of the biblical text by providing historical background information and grammatical and theological interpretation. Each chapter also includes important word lists and questions to enhance and reinforce their learning of the material. My study of Acts has led me to the writings of many people who have profoundly helped to shape my understanding of this book. Consequently, nothing in this book is original with me but is drawn from the contributions of those who have been my teachers.

I must add a special word of appreciation to Zachary Watson for his help in completing this book. His careful proofreading and helpful suggestions significantly improved this book. Moreover, I am profoundly grateful not only for his help in completing this book but also for his kind and gracious spirit.

Abbreviations

KJV	King James Version
NASB	New American Standard Version
NIV	New International Version
NRSV	New Revised Standard
Phillips	The New Testament in Modern English. J. B. Phillips

Introduction to the Acts of the Apostles

The Nature, Purpose, and Thematic Emphasis of Acts

THE BOOK OF ACTS stands at a critical place in the New Testament canon. Acts, the story of the church, stands as a kind of bridge between the Gospels and the Letters. While Acts may have been written after Paul's letters and at least the Gospel of Mark, it deservedly serves as a link between the Gospels and these pastoral texts. Acts gives the reader a context for understanding something about the rise and development of primitive Christianity, not only in its own historical narrative but by assisting the reader to set many of Paul's writings in a particular historical, social, and cultural setting. While there is debate among scholars as to the degree of historical reliability one might give to Acts, most if not all would agree that Acts has helped with the dating of at least some of Paul's writings and the time of his ministry.

Acts has been very influential in shaping believers' understanding of primitive Christianity, which for many believers serves as model, if not a paradigm, for the character and ministry of the church for any age. The assumption has been for many believers that if Acts portrayed the early Christians doing something, then believers in all ages must follow that example, whether it was speaking in tongues, adult believer's baptism, appointment of elders in congregations, the use of church conferences, or the tradition of Sunday assemblies. Of course, Christians have often disagreed regarding what the early church did and what must be repeatable in every generation, and as long as Acts is read and interpreted as primarily a book of laws, disciples of Christ will continue to disagree as to what the church must do or be. This observation doesn't mean that Acts cannot or should not in any way contribute to shaping the community of Jesus; in fact, it can and should do just that. How Acts is formative for the church is the critical concern.

The assumption of this little book is that one must read Acts on its own terms, which means one must determine what the purpose and agenda of the author was. It also means that the truth of Acts may be accessed more from a literary and theological analysis than by the legalistic approaches alluded to above. While it is impossible to go back in time and either dialogue with the author of Acts or, even more, get inside the writer's head, the reader can look for clues in the text that point to matters of emphasis or particular interest to the author. Sometimes, literary styles and context can indicate as to why something is said the way it is, which can suggest an interest or theological orientation of the author. This doesn't imply that the reader should ignore apostolic imperatives or church example—God forbid. These should be taken with great seriousness. Nevertheless, it is essential to read Acts as theological literature or as a theologically interpreted narrative.

A helpful way to highlight this point is to summarize a few theological emphases and literary characteristics of Acts:

Acts: A Continuation of Luke

The historic belief of the church is that Acts and the Third Gospel were written by the same person, Luke, whom Paul described as the beloved physician. The question of authorship will be addressed later, but at this point it can be stated with confidence that the Third Gospel (henceforth referred to as Luke) and Acts were written by the same person. There are linguistic and theological similarities between these two works that will be noted in another section. Significant indicators of common authorship are the two prologues.

> Since many have undertaken to set down an orderly account of the events that have been fulfilled among us, ² just as they were handed on to us by those who from the beginning were eyewitnesses and servants of the word, ³ I too decided, after investigating everything carefully from the very first, ¹ to write an orderly account for you, most excellent Theophilus, ⁴ so that you may know the truth concerning the things about which you have been instructed. (Luke 1:1–4)
>
> In the first book, Theophilus, I wrote about all that Jesus did and taught from the beginning ² until the day when he was taken up

Introduction to the Acts of the Apostles

> to heaven, after giving instructions through the Holy Spirit to the apostles whom he had chosen. ³ After his suffering he presented himself alive to them by many convincing proofs, appearing to them during forty days and speaking about the kingdom of God. (Acts 1:1–3)

First, the "first book" was written concerning the events that occurred "among us," i.e., the Christian community. In other words, Luke's first book was ultimately about the church. Obviously, Acts is also about the church.

Second, in Luke and Acts the writer addresses a certain Theophilus. The identity of this Theophilus is unknown, but since Luke describes him as "most excellent" it has been suggested Theophilus might have been a person in high office, such as a Roman official before whom prisoner Paul might have testified. However, "most excellent Theophilus" might simply have been a person of some distinction. Nevertheless, the commonly named recipient points to a common author. Third, Acts begins with a reference to his first book, a seemingly clear reference to the Gospel of Luke. Moreover, Acts states that in his first book he "wrote about all that Jesus did and taught from the beginning ² until the day when he was taken up to heaven, after giving instructions through the Holy Spirit to the apostles whom he had chosen" (Acts 1:1–2, NRSV). However, the NIV is closer to the meaning of the Greek: "In my former book, Theophilus, I wrote about all that Jesus began to do and to teach ² until the day he was taken up to heaven, after giving instructions through the Holy Spirit to the apostles he had chosen." In the NIV the author states that his first book was concerning "all that Jesus began to do and to teach." This implies the first book was about the ministry of the flesh and blood Jesus and that Acts is about the continuing ministry of the risen Jesus through the church. Consequently, it is fair to describe Acts as the second volume of a two-volume story of the beginning of Christianity.

The Story of the Worldwide Expansion of the Church

The programmatic text for Acts is 1:8: "But you will receive power when the Holy Spirit has come upon you; and you will be my witnesses in Jerusalem, in all Judea and Samaria, and to the ends of the earth." In this passage the author introduces the reader to the power of the Holy Spirit in the life of the church, and a calling for followers of Jesus to be witnesses of Jesus—a calling that will result in the growth and expansion of the church throughout the Roman world. In response to the disciples' question about the restoration of the kingdom of God, the risen Jesus promised his disciples that they would be empowered with the Holy Spirit to testify on his behalf, and that the testimony would begin in Jerusalem, continue to all of Judea and Samaria, and finally reach to the ends of the world (i.e., Rome). Moreover, the predicted geographical spread of the gospel actually suggests a three-part division of the book:

1. The Gospel in Jerusalem (1:1—8:3)
2. The Gospel in Judea, Samaria, Caesarea, and Antioch of Syria (8:4—12:25)
3. The Gospel in Antioch Syria, Asia Minor, Macedonia, Greece, and Rome (chs. 13–28)Another way to see the emphasis on the growth and spread of the gospel in Acts is by noting the author's growth summary statements, or "progress reports," which may also serve as conclusions to sections.

    a. The Church in Jerusalem (1:12—6:6) Progress Report (6:7):

    The word of God continued to spread; the number of the disciples increased greatly in Jerusalem, and a great many of the priests became obedient to the faith.

    b. The Spread of the Church throughout Palestine (6:8—9:30) Progress Report (9:31):

    Meanwhile the church throughout Judea, Galilee, and Samaria had peace and was built up. Living in the fear of the Lord and in the comfort of the Holy Spirit, it increased in numbers.

    c. Extension to Antioch (9:32—12:23) Progress Report (12:24):

    But the word of God continued to advance and gain adherents.

    d. Advance from Syria to Asia (12:25—16:4) Progress Report (16:5):

    So the churches were strengthened in the faith and increased in numbers daily.

    e. Christianity in Europe (16:6—19:9) Progress Report (19:20):

    So the word of the Lord grew mightily and prevailed.

f. Paul's Arrival in Rome and Events that Led to It (19:20—28:30) Progress Report (28:31):

> proclaiming the kingdom of God and teaching about the Lord Jesus Christ with all boldness and without hindrance.

From this analysis it is clear that the author was very interested in the numerical growth of the church and its spread throughout the world, even to the very heart of the Roman Empire.

An Argument for the Full Inclusion of the Gentiles into the Church

The idea of the universalization of the gospel was anticipated in the "first book," or the Third Gospel (Luke 2:29-32; 3:4-6; 4:16-30; 7:1-10), but it has been developed more fully in Acts. In Acts there are three stories that are told or referred to at least three times: (1) the conversion/calling of Saul of Tarsus (Paul); (2) the conversion of Cornelius, the Roman centurion; and (3) the decision of the Jerusalem conference. All three stories are directly related to the matter of the inclusion of Gentiles. The fact that these stories are told, retold or alluded to suggests that the theme of the universal nature and mission of the church is critically important for Acts.

Even the very organizational structure of Acts suggests a universal vision. The gospel begins in Jerusalem and ends in Rome. Moreover, the reader will quickly notice the gradual expansion of the borders of this new Jesus movement. After Jerusalem is evangelized, the story focuses on the evangelization of the people on the margins of Judaism, both in the story of Philip in Samaria and also Philip and the Ethiopian eunuch (Acts 8). Then when Saul of Tarsus is converted, he is called to be a witness to the Gentiles (Acts 9). Following Saul's conversion, Peter converts Cornelius the centurion, who was a Roman (10:1—11:18). After this, Luke turns to the story of the founding of the church in Antioch of Syria, a community of Gentile and Jewish believers, the first integrated church (11:19-30). In chapter 13, the focus of the narrator then turns to the missionary journeys of Paul, efforts which not only proclaimed the gospel to places throughout the Mediterranean world but accelerated the number of non-Jews in the church (Acts 13-14, 16-20). This new reality for some was disturbing, and it led to the conference in Jerusalem that discussed and debated the status of Gentile believers in the fellowship of Jesus. The conclusion of the conference was that Gentiles were not obligated to keep the Mosaic Law as a condition of salvation. Acts concludes with Paul in Rome as a prisoner continuing to testify on behalf of Jesus and the gospel. This survey of Acts shows the Christian church becoming a worldwide community that welcomed all people, both men and women, from all races, nationalities, and social positions. For Luke, this new international fellowship of Jesus followers may have been recognized as the newly redefined, expanded, and restored kingdom of Israel.

The Jewish Rejection and Opposition to the Gospel

According to Acts, the Christian movement was born in Jerusalem. This made sense, since Jesus and all his first disciples, including the Twelve, were Jewish. Yet, one of Acts' consistent themes is that despite this common ground and heritage of faith, and the successful conversion of many Jews to Jesus in the early days, the temple and synagogue authorities, for the most part, rejected the gospel and actively opposed this movement. In most of the stories, the Jewish temple and synagogue leaders were the ones who reject, oppose, and even persecute the followers of Jesus. Some form of opposition or persecution by Jews is recorded in Acts 4:1–31; 5:17–42; 6:8–15; 7:54–60; 8:1–3; 12:1–5; 13:44–46; 14:1–2, 19–20; 17:1–9; 18:12–17; 19:8–10; and chs. 21–24. This opposition is explained in various ways. First, disciples of Christ were persecuted because their savior had previously been persecuted and even killed in part by the same people who were opposing them. Second, the Jewish opposition to the church was provoked by the church's perceived abandonment of their Jewish heritage and faith: they were accused of denigrating the temple, they worshipped a cursed and crucified leader, and—possibly worst of all—they welcomed non-Jews to fellowship with no requirement of circumcision or any other Mosaic Law. Belief in the resurrection, especially the resurrection of Jesus, only exacerbated the theological debate because it seemed to imply God's endorsement of these "heretical" innovations. After all, if Jesus has been raised, he must really be the Messiah.

Christianity Is Not Against Judaism but Is Its True Expression

In the sermons in Acts, there is a consistent argument that the gospel does not negate the faith of Israel but instead fulfills it. In accordance with this,

Peter quotes from Joel in his Pentecost sermon, and the Psalms stress Jesus as the fulfillment of the promises of God. Even Jesus' death and resurrection were predicted in the Hebrew Scriptures. Furthermore, in one of Paul's main sermons he strongly argued that God has been at work among his people since the days of Moses to accomplish his plan, culminating with the coming of the savior Jesus, God's Son. Also, when Paul spoke in defense of himself before the Jews and Roman authorities, he consistently emphasized that he continued to believe what the Law and the Prophets had written long ago, particularly concerning the Messiah and his resurrection. Paul did not regard himself as a former Jew, but as a Jew who believed in Jesus. Acts' version of the messages of Peter and Paul, the two primary spokespersons for the primitive church, is that Christianity was the true fulfillment of the faith of Israel because they believed Jesus to be the promised Messiah to Israel and savior of the world.

The Power of the Holy Spirit in the Life of the Church

As noted above, the power of the Holy Spirit is one of the prominent themes in Acts. Not only is it mentioned in 1:8, but it appears numerous times throughout this book. The church is born with the outpouring of the Holy Spirit, which not only empowered the disciples to speak in tongues but allowed Peter to deliver a powerful first sermon. Repeatedly, the Holy Spirit is portrayed as directing and empowering the ministries. In 8:39 the Spirit instructed Philip to get in the chariot and teach the Ethiopian. The Spirit directed Peter to go the house of Cornelius (10:19). The leaders of the Antioch church decided to appoint Barnabas and Saul to missionary work at the direction of the Spirit (13:1–3). The Spirit guided the Jerusalem conference in their decision to accept Gentiles as full and equal members in the fellowship (15:28). It was also the Spirit that directed Paul on his missionary journey sometimes by preventing him from going in a certain direction (16:6). Even the elders of the Ephesians received their appointment through the guidance of the Spirit (20:28). This brief overview shows that, for Luke, the Holy Spirit was the power and inspiration for the church's life and work.

Jesus Is the Living Lord of the Church

There is no more constant theme in Acts than the proclamation of the resurrection of Jesus. In every major apostolic speech in Acts, the resurrection of Jesus is not only mentioned but is usually the centerpiece of the remarks. While Luke understands the death of Jesus to be salvific, there is very little emphasis in Luke or Acts on the atonement. For example, only twice in Acts is there mention of the blood of Jesus (in 5:28 by opponents of Jesus and the apostles, and in 20:28 by Paul, who said the church had been purchased by Jesus' blood). Instead of blood atonement, Acts regards the resurrection of Jesus as the theological center of the gospel.

In addition to multiple references about the resurrection in speeches, Acts also narrates several appearances of the risen Jesus to disciples and, especially, Paul. Acts opens with the risen Jesus appearing to the apostles for forty days, during which he gives instruction concerning the kingdom of God (1:1–7). Also, there are three accounts of Saul or Paul encountering the risen Jesus while on the road to Damascus (9:4–5; 22:4–16; 26:9–18). Additionally, Jesus appears to Paul during his second missionary journey while in Corinth (18:9–10), during his first visit to Jerusalem after his conversion (22:17–18), and while he is in prison in Jerusalem (23:11). Finally, one interesting characteristic of Acts is that all the healings done by the apostles are attributed to Jesus, to faith in Jesus, or to the name of Jesus. Moreover, some of the healing stories seem to echo the healings of Jesus in the Gospels. The point here is that Acts seems to be suggesting that the miracles of the apostles are really the miracles of Jesus through the apostles: the continuing ministry of Jesus, who is now risen.

Peter and Paul

It has been widely noted that in Acts 1–12, roughly the first half of the book, the dominant human figure is Peter. In Acts 13–28, though, the dominant person is Paul. Acts portrays the ministries of Peter and Paul very similarly. For example, each presents very important speeches to Jews and Gentiles, each is imprisoned and miraculously delivered, each defends himself before the Sanhedrin, each raises someone from the dead, and each delivers a stinging rebuke of an unbelieving magus. The parallel portrayals of the ministries of Peter and Paul must be for a reason. The most common explanation is that Luke was favorably comparing Paul with Peter. For those who believe Luke/Acts was written in the early 60s, this insight may mean Acts sought to legitimatize Paul's apostleship by showing he was every bit equal to Peter. For those who date Acts after 80 and possibly near the second century, the comparison of Paul with Peter is less about the individual apostles and more about the reconciliation of Pauline and Petrine communities of faith. Whichever view one may take, it should be noted that, for the author of Acts, Paul is the real human hero of his story.

Conclusion

There are other suggested themes for Acts, which, however plausible, are not pertinent for this study. Obviously, since Acts records several defense speeches by Paul and ends with Paul in house arrest in Rome, some have been tempted to suggest that Acts served as some kind of defense for Paul when he was in Rome. Others have argued that Acts' focus on the ministry of the church with little emphasis on the second coming suggests that the author conceived of the church at a time when there was little anticipation of an imminent return of Jesus. Thus the church is called to faithfully wait and carry out her mission.

One final thought: Historically the church has regarded this work as the Acts of the Apostles. That is still the traditional title given in most Bibles. However, Acts' strong emphasis on the power of the Holy Spirit in the life of the church and on Jesus as the living Lord of the church requires that readers regard this work as the Acts of Jesus in the church through the power of the Holy Spirit. Ultimately, Acts is the story of how God accomplished his mission through the ongoing ministry of the living Jesus in the church. He is the real hero of the story of Acts.

The Authorship and Date of Acts

Authorship

It should first be noted that both the Gospel of Luke and the book of Acts are anonymous works. The superscriptions for both of these works were clearly added sometime during the second century and should be taken seriously as a very early opinion concerning these works. In fact, the unanimous testimony of the early church fathers was that Luke was the author of Luke and Acts. By the third century, the Lucan authorship of Luke/Acts was undisputed.

Even though Acts does not identify by name the author, it may give some clues. The most significant clues are the well-known "we" passages (16:10–17; 20:5—21:18; 27:1—28:16). The traditional interpretation of the first-person plural pronoun found in these texts is that the writer of these passages had been a companion of Paul and an eyewitness to some of Paul's experiences. Taken at face value, the "we" passages suggest that the author joined Paul during his second missionary journey, probably at Troas, and traveled with Paul to Philippi in Macedonia. These "we" passages disappear after Paul leaves Philippi (16:18), which may suggest that the author stayed in Philippi. Then the "we" passages reappear in the section concerning Paul's third missionary journey (20:5), where it states a group of believers had been "waiting for us in Troas." Paul had left Philippi to return to Troas (20:6), implying the author had rejoined Paul in Philippi and traveled with the apostle as he returned to Jerusalem, completing his third missionary journey. The final occurrences of the "we" passages are in 27:1—28:16, which narrate Paul's voyage, shipwreck, and arrival at Rome, which means the author was an eyewitness to these events. Seven men from Beroea, Thessalonica, Derbe, and Asia traveled with Paul on his return to Jerusalem (20:4). Curiously, there is no mention of any representative from Philippi, which seemed to have been an important center of the Pauline mission. If the "we" passage in 20:8 suggests that the author had been in Philippi, perhaps he was Philippi's representative.

Yet if one assumes the author of the "we" passages to be the author of Acts and even embraces the conjecture that the author may have been Philippi's representative traveling with Paul, the name of the author is still a mystery. The only name that has been suggested for the authorship of the third Gospel and Acts is a person called Luke. There are only three passages in the New Testament that clearly mention a Christian associate of Paul named Luke: Philemon 24, which mentions Luke as a "fellow worker"; Colossians 4:10–14, which implies Luke is an uncircumcised Gentile; and 2 Timothy 4:11, which states Luke was with Paul in prison. Interestingly, all three of these texts claim to have been written by Paul in prison, traditionally assumed to have been in Rome. Since the author of the "we" passages in Acts 27–28 traveled with Paul to Rome, it is reasonable to conclude that he also was in prison with Paul in Rome at this time. Admittedly, information concerning Luke is limited and does not compel the interpreter to identify him as the author of Acts. So, is the identity of Luke as the author of Luke/Acts consistent with the evidence in both Acts and the letters of Paul? Many scholars would say yes, but not everyone. Since the nineteenth century, there have been arguments presented that raised considerable doubt concerning Luke's authorship of Acts. The arguments generally center on perceived historical discrepancies between Acts and the letters of Paul. The opponents of Luke's authorship contend that the author of Acts could not have been a close companion of Paul since his portrait of Paul is radically different from that found in the letters. For example, Paul in Acts seems more accepting of Jewish law when he had Timothy circumcised because of the Jews (Acts 16:1–3) than he does in the letters when he refused to circumcise Titus to placate the traditionalists (Gal 2:1–5). Other perceived discrepancies are the nature and decision of the Jerusalem conference and Paul's conversion. It has also been suggested that the author of Acts distorted history by smoothing out the theological differences between Jewish and Gentile Christians. An argument here is that in Acts once the Jerusalem conference makes its decision of welcoming Gentiles and communicates this to all the churches, theological conflict within churches ceases, yet Paul's letters show continuing disagreement concerning the relationship of Gentile and Jewish believers. Furthermore, it has also been pointed out that Luke doesn't mention any of Paul's letters, with which he must have been familiar.

These so-called discrepancies may be more apparent than real. For example, it is now widely acknowledged that while Paul proclaimed a righteousness apart from the Law of Moses, Paul never rejected his Jewish heritage or the Jewish Law. Moreover, one must keep in mind the contexts where there seem to be historical differences. For example, the contexts that provoked Paul to prohibit circumcision at one time and insist on it in another were quite different. Also, the fact that Acts and Paul describe what seems to be the Jerusalem conference in quite different ways does not necessarily imply contradiction but differences in emphasis in the two versions of that event. The same can also be said regarding the different accounts of Paul's conversion.

Beside the historical argument, others have pointed to the strikingly similar style and vocabulary in all the speeches in Acts supposedly given by different people. The argument here is that these so-called speeches are not actually speeches by Peter, Stephen, and Paul, but literary creations of the author, something an eyewitness would not have done. Thus, if Luke was the author, he most likely would not have been an eyewitness to speeches of Peter and Stephen and would have had to rely on eyewitness accounts. Clearly, though, the speeches are not complete transcripts, for they are too short. They are most likely summaries or distillations of the original orations. If this is the case, it would not be surprising if the author took those elements that he deemed important—e.g., Jesus' resurrection—and reshaped them in his own language. In this way, the author's hand would be involved in the composition of these speeches while maintaining faithfulness to what was originally spoken. If this explanation is true, there is no reason Luke could not have been the author. So, while certainty concerning the authorship of Acts is not possible, it is reasonable to conclude that the author was Luke, the beloved physician and missionary companion of Paul. Therefore, the Lucan authorship of Luke and Acts has been assumed in this volume.

The Date of Composition

Luke does not specifically tell the reader when he wrote Acts. Obviously, Acts was written after what he called his "first book," i.e., the Third Gospel, and after Paul was placed in house arrest in Rome, which likely took place between 60 and 62.

There are three controlling factors in determining the date of composition. First, one must decide whether or not Luke knew or borrowed from the Gospel of Mark in the composition of his Gospel. The widely accepted two-source theory of the Synoptic Gospels assumes that Mark was the first Gospel to be written and that Matthew and Luke drew from Mark in the writing of their respective works. Church tradition and most scholars assign a date of Mark no earlier than around 65 and generally no later than 75. If these dates are correct, then if Luke borrowed from or knew of Mark, he could not have written Luke and Acts before 65 and likely wrote closer to 80–85.

Second, one must decide whether or not the conclusion of Acts with Paul in prison is a clue to the date of composition. Since Acts gives no information concerning the outcome of Paul's appeal after he arrived in Rome, some have suggested that Acts must have been written while Paul was still under house arrest, awaiting a decision by the emperor. That would mean that Acts was written around 62. However, if one reads Acts as a theologically interpreted narrative, then one may conclude that the result of Paul's appeal was not a concern of the writer. The goal in Acts is to get the gospel to Rome, and it does so through the prisoner Paul. The fact that Paul may or may not have been acquitted and released is not important to the story; what is important is that Paul testifies of Jesus in the heart of the Roman Empire. So, the ending of Acts may have been influenced more by theological than historical concerns. Even if Acts was written in the 60s, the ending of the book is really a non-factor in determining the date of composition. Other matters must be taken into consideration.

Third, one must determine whether Acts was written shortly after the events described or as if these were events from the distant past. Taking

Luke and Acts together, some scholars claim to have found clues to a late date for Acts (90–100). Some of their arguments are based on the following: (1) the highly organized structure of Luke/Acts into two volumes, each with a prologue; (2) the apparent end of Jew/Gentile controversy; (3) interest in Christian psalmody; (4) interest in church organization; (5) concern for false teaching; (6) apparent ignorance of Paul's letters; (7) presupposition of the wide success of the Gentile mission.

One's opinion on the date of Acts does not significantly impact the interpretation of this book. However, since it is very likely that Luke knew of and drew from Mark in the writing of his Gospel, the date of composition was most likely not before 80, but probably not as late as 100. A date of composition during the decade of the 80s and possibly early 90s is the present author's best estimate.

For Further Study

Questions

1. People have tended to read Acts in three ways: (1) as a description of what happened or what was said; (2) as a guideline or model for what the church or Christians should do or believe; (3) as a literary work that artistically and theologically conveys important truths. Read Acts 2:41–47. How should this text be read? Choose from one of the three methods summarized above and give a reason for your position.

2. Which of the themes/purposes of Acts did you find the most compelling, interesting, or even surprising? Why?

3. Does it make any difference who wrote Acts and when it was written?

ACTS 1

The Preparation for the Coming of the Holy Spirit

Introduction (Acts 1:1–5)

WHILE THE AUTHOR OF Acts (I shall henceforth call him Luke) opens with no explicitly stated purpose for writing, it is clear that he assumed the purpose of his first volume, the Gospel of Luke. Not only did Luke, as in his Gospel, identify Theophilus as the recipient of Acts, he also wrote his story of the early years of the church in an orderly and logical manner. In Acts 1:1, Luke describes his Gospel as a book "about all that Jesus began to do and to teach." If the Third Gospel was about the beginning of Jesus' ministry, then it follows that Acts is about the ongoing ministry of Jesus. Put in another way, Luke's Gospel is the story of the ministry of Jesus in the flesh, while his second volume, Acts, is the story of the ministry Jesus in the Spirit as it was carried out by the church.

Acts 1:2–5 summarizes the resurrection appearances of Jesus to the apostles. Luke states that Jesus gave instructions through the Holy Spirit. This personally powerful presence of the Spirit, which empowered Christ, would be also given to the church to help it carry out its mission in the world. Moreover, according to Acts, Jesus appeared to the apostles for forty days. The Greek text literally means "through days days," and this suggests these were probably repeated appearances where Jesus appeared, disappeared, and later reappeared to them over a period of forty days, instead of one continual resurrection appearance that lasted forty days. During this forty-day period, Luke states that Jesus spoke about the kingdom of God. While the content of these instructions are not given, most likely they included references to Old Testament prophecies concerning the kingdom, the nature of the kingdom, and the meaning of one's life under the rule of God (see Luke 6:20–49; 10:25–37; 14:1–24; 15:1–32; 16:1–31;17:20–37). According to Israel's prophets, one of the signs of the coming of the kingdom would be the powerful activity of the Spirit of God in the world and among God's people. Consistent with this, Jesus promised that his disciples would be empowered with the Holy Spirit. He noted that John the Baptist had predicted that the Messiah would baptize with the Holy Spirit (Luke 3:3–18). Whatever John had meant by his words, for Jesus and his followers they came to refer to the outpouring of God's Spirit, which signaled the breaking in of God's kingdom and the birth of the church. In preparation for this powerful new work of God, Jesus instructed the apostles to wait, probably in prayer, for the promised Holy Spirit of God.

Commission of the Apostles (Acts 1:6–8)

Sometime during this forty-day period, the disciples asked Jesus if he was about to restore the kingdom to Israel. Jesus' disciples seemed to have had two concerns in their question. First, they apparently desired to know when the kingdom would be established. This is a question of timing, not unlike some Christians' concern about the second coming of Jesus. Second, the disciples expressed interest in Israel's relation to the restored kingdom. The theme of the restoration of the kingdom appears in other places in Luke-Acts as part of the hope of Israel. The following quotations show the importance of this theme:

> Now there was a man in Jerusalem whose name was Simeon; this man was righteous and devout, looking forward to the consolation of Israel, and the Holy Spirit rested on him. (Luke 2:25)

> At that moment she came, and began to praise God and to speak about the child to all who were looking for the redemption of Jerusalem. (Luke 2:38)

> The things about Jesus of Nazareth, who was a prophet mighty in deed and word before God and all the people, 20 and how our chief priests and leaders handed him over to be condemned to death and crucified him. 21 But we had hoped that he was the one to redeem Israel. (Luke 24:19b–21a)

> Repent therefore, and turn to God so that your sins may be wiped out, 20 so that times of refreshing may come from the presence of the Lord, and that he may send the Messiah appointed for you, that is, Jesus, 21 who must remain in heaven until the time of universal restoration that God announced long ago through his holy prophets. (Acts 3:19–21)

The Old Testament story of the kingdom of Israel begins with the reign of Saul, followed by David and David's son Solomon. Only these three kings reigned over a united Israelite kingdom. Shortly after Solomon's death, Israel suffered a civil war that split the kingdom into two: the Kingdom of Israel located in the north, and the Kingdom of Judah in the south. When the two rival kingdoms fell to the more powerful nations of Assyria and later Babylon, and its people were driven into exile, the prophets began to speak of the time when divided Israel would be reunited and established as one kingdom, ruled by a descendant of David, thought of by some as the Anointed One or the Messiah (see Ezek 37:15–28).

Jesus did not initially correct the disciples' apparent mistaken understanding of an earthly kingdom. Rather he first reminds them that God is in control of the timing of the kingdom's restoration. Then he commissioned them to testify of him "in Jerusalem, and all Judea and Samaria, and to the ends of the earth," as they are empowered with the Holy Spirit (Acts 1:8). Three important themes for Acts are introduced in this verse. First, the primary work of the apostles, and later the church as a whole, is to witness or testify. The heart of this testimony was the story of Jesus, culminating in his unjust death and triumphant resurrection. Second, the ability of the church to effectively witness to Jesus would be made possible through the power of the Holy Spirit. Third, the geographical progression "Jerusalem, and all Judea and Samaria, and to the ends of the earth" outlines the universal nature of the church's mission. In fact, Acts is organized in accordance with this geographical progression: (1) Jerusalem, Acts 1:1—8:3; (2) Judea and Samaria, Acts 8:4—12:25; and (3) ends of the earth, Acts 13:1—28:31. Additionally, each of these three geographical designations is theologically significant for the apostles' mission. First, the mission obviously begins in Jerusalem, the city of David and the place both of the rejection of the Messiah and the beginning of the new age of the Spirit, the age of salvation. Second, Judea and Samaria are not only names of two neighboring rival territories, but were once the names of the two rival Jewish kingdoms: Judah and Samaria or Israel. The phrase "all Judea and Samaria" should be interpreted as referring to one activity. Jesus did not say they were to witness in Judea and then Samaria, but that they were to witness in Judea and Samaria as if it were one region. Like many of the prophets of old, Luke conceived of one united (or reunited) Israel. The apostles witnessing to both regions and bringing believers from both Judea and Samaria into this new believing community would signify the beginning of the reunification of the ancient kingdom of Israel, thus beginning the restoration of the kingdom. Third, the church was to witness "to the ends of the earth." This final geographical designation shows the international and diverse nature of God's restored kingdom. In the days of the nation of Israel, the kingdom of God was identified with Israel. However, Jesus stated that the restored Israel will spread all over the world and include people of all races and cultures. This third division takes up more than half the book of Acts (13–28), which means that the international and inclusive makeup of the church is the primary concern of the author. For Luke, the gospel is meant for all people.

The Ascension of Jesus (Acts 1: 9–11)

When Jesus had finished his words to the disciples, Acts states that "he was taken up before their very eyes, and a cloud hid him from their sight." The story of Jesus' ascension is similar to the Old Testament stories concerning Enoch and Elijah. The Genesis writer states that God took Enoch away because he walked faithfully with God (Gen 5:22–24). Similarly, the prophet Elijah went up to heaven in a whirlwind (2 Kgs 2:11–12). These two unusual events happened to men who were portrayed as righteous and godly. Acts, though, additionally states that "a cloud took him out of their sight." Most likely, this clause means more than Jesus disappeared into a cloud as he ascended. Rather, it could mean that a cloud took action to hide Jesus from their sight. The author is thinking of the pillar of cloud that led Israel in the wilderness (Exod 16:10) and also the cloud that appeared at Jesus' baptism and later at his transfiguration: the cloud sometimes referred to as the Shekinah glory, the glorious presence of God wrapped and veiled in mystery and clouds. Taken this way, Luke is saying that it was God who took Jesus and hid him from the apostles' sight.

The significance of this event is not that Jesus simply was miraculously levitated from the earth's surface to the mysterious realm of heaven in the sky. When one considers that the earth is a globe that circles the sun in the midst of this vast universe, the meaning of a person ascending "up" from the earth takes on a different meaning. However, for Acts, the ascension is not about physical direction but spiritual transition and exaltation. The claim of Acts is that Jesus was lifted off the surface of the earth and was taken by God to the spiritual dimensions of heaven, where he was and is exalted at the right hand of God himself. Peter says as much in his Pentecost sermon:

> "This Jesus God raised up, and of that all of us are witnesses. [33] Being therefore exalted at the right hand of God, and having received from the Father the promise of the Holy Spirit, he has poured out this that you both see and hear. [34] For David did not ascend into the heavens, but he himself says,
> 'The Lord said to my Lord, "Sit at my right hand,
> [35] until I make your enemies your footstool."'
> [36] Therefore let the entire house of Israel know with certainty that God has made him both Lord and Messiah, this Jesus whom you crucified." (Acts 2:32–36)

After Jesus ascended, the text states that suddenly two men dressed in white stood beside the apostles and assured them Jesus would someday return. While the two men are generally understood to be angels, they are literally called "men." In Luke's version of the resurrection of Jesus, it says that two men in lightning-bright clothes suddenly stood beside the visiting women and assured them that Jesus had risen from the grave (Luke 24:1–8). In Mark's account, he refers to the messenger (he mentions only one) in white at the empty tomb as a young man (Mark 16:2–7). Matthew, though, refers to an angel (one angel) of the Lord (Matt 28:2–7), and John to two angels (John 20:11–12). The thrust of the angels' message to the apostles is that the *same* Jesus who left will return and that his second coming will be like the ascension. In other words, Jesus' second coming will be personal (he himself will come) and his return will be dramatic and visible like his departure.

The Disciples Waiting in Jerusalem (Acts 1:12–14)

In obedience to Jesus' instruction, the apostles returned to Jerusalem to wait for the fulfillment of God's empowering presence. Luke says that the distance from the Mount of Olives, the apparent site of the ascension, to Jerusalem was a Sabbath day's journey, which is approximately three thousand feet or a little more than half a mile. When they arrived, they went to the upper room of a house (possibly the place of the Last Supper) and spent time in prayer. This gathering included the apostles minus Judas Iscariot, Mary the mother of Jesus, a group called "the women," and the brothers of Jesus. "The women" were likely the same group of women disciples who both followed Jesus and financially supported him during his ministry (Luke 8:1–4) and likely included the first eyewitnesses to the empty tomb of Jesus (Luke 24:1–10). Most likely, this group was praying for God to send the promised Holy Spirit, which would signify the arrival of the reign of God.

The Selection of Matthias to Replace Judas (Acts 1:15–26)

Even though the gathering in the upper room may have seemed rather small—possibly around 20 persons—before long the group had grown to about 120. Obviously, the group had moved from the small confines of the upper room to a larger area, possibly a section in the temple area. In this scene, Peter emerges as the recognized leader of this fledgling band of believers. The apostle's first task is to guide the group to choose a replacement for Judas Iscariot, who had suffered a horrible death following his betrayal of Jesus. Peter points out that the scriptures foretold the events concerning Judas. No Old Testament text is cited, but Peter may have had in mind Psalm 41:9:

> Even my bosom friend in whom I trusted, who ate of my bread,
> has lifted the heel against me. (See John 13:18)

Peter recounts the death of Judas as a sad but fitting end of one so close to Jesus. An account of his death is recorded or summarized only in Matthew 27:3–10 and Acts 1:18. When the two versions are compared, there are some interesting differences as to the cause of Judas' death. According to Matthew, Judas died by hanging himself. On the other hand, according to Acts, Peter states that Judas died by falling headlong and his swollen body bursting open. Some have suggested that what really happened is that Judas hung himself, after which his body later burst apart when decay set in. This theory conflates the two separate versions to present what is considered as a plausible explanation for the differences. Another possible interpretation is that Matthew presents a literal description of Judas' death and that Acts presents a literary interpretation of it. Actually, the differences between Matthew and Acts are very minor. Both versions portray the death as self-inflicted and state that the field where he died was later named "Field of Blood." The thrust of Matthew's version is to show the tragedy of a man who realized the gravity of his sin and couldn't live with himself, whereas Peter in Acts seems to stress the utter dishonor and shame associated with Judas' death as just punishment for his sin against the Lord. To elaborate on the shame of Judas, Peter cites two passages from the Psalms. The first is Psalm 69:25: "May *their* camp be a desolation; let no one live in *their* tents." This quotation is altered slightly in Acts, for it reads: "Let *his* homestead become desolate, and let there be no one to live in it." Peter changes the plural pronoun ("their") for a singular pronoun ("his") to apply this text directly to Judas. The second text is Psalm 109:8: "May his days be few; may another take his place of leadership." The word for "leadership" comes from the Greek word *episkopos*, which is also translated as "bishop" or "overseer" (Ps 109:8).

It might be asked why the apostles felt it necessary to replace Judas. Why not carry on Jesus' mission as the eleven apostles? It is generally agreed that since the number twelve was an important symbol for Israel, the twelve apostles were a symbol of the new or renewed Israel that Jesus established. Yet, this is the only time that a replacement was done. When the apostle James was executed in Acts 12, Acts does not indicate that the remaining apostles chose a replacement for James. The explanation must be that since the primary mission of the twelve apostles was to testify of Jesus of Nazareth, especially his death and resurrection, that even though James had fallen in death, his life and message remained a testimony to Jesus, whereas Judas' betrayal of Jesus disqualified him as one of the testifying apostles.

Peter makes it very clear that the Twelve, as they were commonly known, functioned as the authoritative and primary witnesses to the life, ministry, death, burial, and resurrection of Jesus. That is why any candidate for the ministry of apostle must be one who had been with Jesus and the other apostles from the beginning of Jesus' ministry until the ascension. In fact, Peter explicitly says that the apostles are to function as witnesses of Jesus' resurrection. It is interesting that in Acts Paul is never portrayed as, nor claims to be, either a replacement or the thirteenth apostle. He was simply a different kind of apostle.

The selection process was a mixture of human judgment and divine guidance. After a process of elimination of potential candidates, two men remained as the potential replacement apostle: Judas, also known as Barsabbas, and Matthias. Acts states that the group first prayed that the Lord would point out to them the right person. Then, drawing from an early form of gambling, the text says the group cast lots. On the surface this appears to show the group relying on chance to determine the next apostle. However, since their action followed a time of prayer for guidance, it can be assumed that the group believed God would reveal his choice through the casting of lots. The lot fell on Matthais as the new apostle. Strangely, Luke never again mentions Matthais in this narrative. Perhaps Acts is subtlety recalling Israel's priests' use of the Urim and the Thummin as a way to discern God's will (Exod 28:29–30; Num 27:31).

For Further Study

Important Names or Terms

- Theophilus
- Kingdom of God
- Witness
- Apostle
- Matthais
- Barsabbas

Questions

1. How did the disciples conceive the restoration of the kingdom to Israel? Did the writer of Acts understand the restoration of the kingdom differently than the disciples? If yes, in what way?
2. What were the requirements for someone to be appointed as one of the twelve apostles? Why are those requirements so important?
3. What can be learned about the role and function of the Holy Spirit from Acts 1?
4. What function does prayer have for these early believers in Jesus?

ACTS 2:1—8:3

The Church in Jerusalem

ACTS 2

The Coming of the Holy Spirit and the Birth of the Church

Pentecost and the Outpouring of the Holy Spirit (Acts 2:1–13)

ACTS 2, WITH THE outpouring of the Holy Spirit, the preaching of Peter, and the conversion of at least three thousand people, is for Christians the foundational text for the church. These events have been referred to collectively in several ways, including "the birth of Christianity." In fact, Acts repeatedly looks back and/or alludes to this event as that which gave identity and shape to this young messianic movement.

The Feast of Pentecost was a harvest festival that took place fifty days from the beginning of Passover and lasted for one week. It was also known as the Feast of Weeks, since fifty days was seven weeks plus one day from Passover. In the first century, Pentecost, along with Passover and Tabernacles, was one of the three great pilgrim festivals of the Jews, thus thousands of pious Jews from around the world gathered in the city of David to collectively worship the God of Israel. Originally, Pentecost was established as a festival of joy and thanksgiving for the blessings of the harvest. All work was to be suspended so that people could come to the temple to worship. Expressions of praise and thanksgiving were made, and sin and peace offerings were offered daily (Lev 23:15–22; Deut 16:9–12). However, it appears that by the first century Pentecost had also become a time of celebration for God's gift of the Law along with the establishment of the covenant. For Luke it may be more than ironic that the inauguration of the new covenant through Jesus took place at the time when Israel celebrated the establishment of the first covenant.

The description of the first Christian Pentecost was drawn from the Old Testament prophecies concerning "the Day of the Lord." First, Luke states there was a sound "like" a rushing/violent wind. This sound may not have been literal wind but only sounded like it. It should be noted that the translated words "spirit," "wind," and "breath" come from one word, whether in Hebrew (*ruach*) or Greek (*pneuma*). In the Gospel of John, Jesus spoke of spirit and wind using the same Greek word (John 3:5–8). Acts assumes the reader will understand the sound of wind to signal the coming of the Spirit. Second, the text states that the group saw what "seemed" to be tongues of fire on disciples. Again, the text doesn't say there were actual fiery tongues on the disciples' heads. Rather, it says they saw something that had the appearance of tongues of fire. In other words, this was similar to a visionary experience, which nearly always contains symbolic images. Fire is often a symbol for both judgment and purification. For example, God purified the lips of Isaiah by touching them with fiery coals (Isa 6:6–7). Also, experiences of theophany, or the divine presence, are sometimes described with images of fire.

In Acts 2:4 the writer states, "All of them were filled with the Holy Spirit and began to speak in other languages." The typical way to describe one who had been endowed with the gift and utterance of prophecy was to say he/she had been filled with the Spirit. It is reasonable, therefore, to conclude that the Pentecost crowd heard prophetic speech. In fact, when the members of the crowd declared that they heard them "declaring the wonders of God," they were likely describing words of prophecy. Yet this was not typical speech. It was speech in "other languages as the Spirit gave them ability." The word translated "languages" is the Greek *dialektos*, from which the English word "dialect" is derived. In other words, Luke is describing Spirit speech in several human dialects or languages. The purpose of this miracle was not primarily to communicate a divine message in the languages of many people, who would not have otherwise understood it. After all, since Greek was the international language of the empire, most likely all Peter would have had to do was to speak in Greek and all or most would have understood. If this analysis is correct, then what was the purpose of the miracle? Acts stresses that Jews from all over the world heard the message of these first Christians in their local languages or dialects. For that reason, some believe this miracle was a kind of reversal of the curse of the tower of Babel, the place where God caused the multiplicity of human language (Gen 11:1–9). The significance of this would have been that by overcoming the human barrier of language, the human race can begin to come together as one people united under the lordship of Jesus. This noble ideal is in fact expressed throughout Acts as the universal nature of the gospel becomes clear. Nevertheless, in chapter 2 the author states that those who were gathered from various points in the world were Jews. Perhaps, then, a better explanation of the miracle is to see it as a sign of the reunification of the Jewish people and, thus, as the restoration of the kingdom to Israel.

The enthusiasm of these Spirit-filled disciples caused some on-the-scene skeptics to conclude that they were drunk. While the reference to drunkenness has been interpreted as evidence of ecstatic spiritual experiences, it may simply mean that the enthusiasm of those believers was so dramatic or expressive that some felt compelled to discredit it by ascribing it to drunkenness. The apostle Peter quickly dismissed that charge by pointing out it was only 9:00 in the morning. The literal translation of the time is "the third hour of the day." The Jewish day began at dawn (approximately 6:00 a.m.) and ended at dusk (approximately 6:00 p.m.), so 9:00 a.m. would logically have been far too early for people to be getting drunk.

Acts 2:1–4 states that "they" who were all together heard the sound of the Spirit, saw what appeared as tongues of fire, received the filling, and spoke in tongues. What did Luke mean by the pronoun "they"? In other words, who experienced this filling of the Spirit? For most readers of Acts the answer to this question seems clear: the believers who numbered at least 120 persons were the ones who received the filling of the Spirit. The implication for this interpretation is that the filling of the Spirit was bestowed on all the believers and suggests that Spirit filling is for all Christians. In support of this, it often is pointed out that Peter told the Pentecost crowd that the promised gift of the Spirit was "for you, for your children, and for all who are far away, everyone whom the Lord our God calls to him" (2:39).

However, there is an alternative view that argues that the filling of the Spirit on Pentecost was only given to the twelve apostles. Part of the confusion is Luke's use of the pronoun "they." Clearly, Jesus promised the apostles would receive the Holy Spirit in 1:8. Consequently, it is argued that every occurrence of "they" through 1:14 refers to these chosen followers. Advocates of this second view also point out that the crowd refers to the tongue speakers as "Galileans," which could hardly describe all 120, but would describe the apostles. Moreover, following the Galilean reference,

Acts states that Peter stood up with "the Eleven"; no mention is made of the 120. Finally, since Jesus had promised the Holy Spirit to the apostles to aid in their work as witnesses (1:8), it makes sense to interpret this filling of the Spirit in reference to the apostles only.

In response to the above interpretation, charismatics argue that in 1:23–25 the word "they" could refer to either the Twelve or the 120. So, when Acts 2 mentions "they" were filled with the Spirit and spoke in tongues, it is not clear that Acts has only the Twelve in mind. Also, since Peter said the promise of the Spirit was for all believers, it makes sense to conclude that all the believers had been filled with the Spirit.

This debate is rooted in the disagreement between charismatic and non-charismatic Christians. Charismatic believers, though not only they, point out that Luke portrayed the entire believing community as having been filled with the Spirit and speaking in tongues in order to highlight the belief that the charismatic gifts of the Spirit continue to be part of God's blessing for the church. Some non-charismatic believers restrict the filling in Acts 2 to the apostles because they believe Scripture teaches that the charismatic gifts had a very specific and limited purpose: to confirm the truth of the gospel. Consequently, these interpreters argue that these gifts ceased sometime near the close of the first century, having fulfilled their function and purpose. However, in this writer's opinion, it seems that the spiritual gifts debate does not rest on who were speaking in tongues on the Day of Pentecost. Moreover, though Acts identifies only the apostles in 2:14, this does not mean that the rest had not also been filled with the Spirit, only that the apostles utilized their gifts to fulfill their role as witnesses.

Peter's Sermon at Pentecost (Acts 2:14–36)

Acts states that Peter addressed both the residents of Judea and Jerusalem, along with Jews who had traveled to Jerusalem to celebrate the Feast of Pentecost. Peter opened with the claim that the events the crowds had been witnessing were not signs of drunkenness but signs of the fulfillment of the promises of God to Israel. To demonstrate this, the apostle quoted an oracle from the prophet Joel (Joel 2:28–32). The following is the text as it appears in the Old Testament:

> Then afterward I will pour out my spirit on all flesh; your sons and your daughters shall prophesy, your old men shall dream dreams, and your young men shall see visions. [29] Even on the male and

female slaves, in those days, I will pour out my spirit. ³⁰ I will show portents in the heavens and on the earth, blood and fire and columns of smoke. ³¹ The sun shall be turned to darkness, and the moon to blood, before the great and terrible day of the LORD comes. ³² Then everyone who calls on the name of the LORD shall be saved; for in Mount Zion and in Jerusalem there shall be those who escape, as the LORD has said, and among the survivors shall be those whom the LORD calls.

Peter's quotation of this text is slightly different from the Old Testament oracle and likely is an indication of a Christian reinterpretation of Joel. First, Peter began the quotation with the phrase, "in the last days" (Acts 2:17), whereas Joel reads, "Then afterward." Joel began his oracle with "afterward" because it originally referred to the judgment of God against Israel with a plague of locusts, followed by God's promise to remove the plague and restore fertility to the land; after judgment would follow reconciliation and renewal. However, Peter's insertion of "in the last days" stressed that the Pentecost experience was the pivotal shift of God's work in salvation history. In other words, the "last days" referred to the last age, in which God acts to bring salvation to the world.

There are other changes that Peter made to Joel's prophecy. First, the phrase "and they shall prophesy" (Acts 2:18) is not in Joel. This appears to be an emphasis on the Spirit being poured out on *all people* from *all stations of life*. Second, where Joel wrote, "portents in the heavens and on the earth" (Joel 2:30), Peter stated, "portents in the heaven above and signs on the earth below" (Acts 2:19). Third, after the clause "everyone who calls on the name of the Lord will be saved," Acts omits the rest of Joel 2:32: "for in Mount Zion and in Jerusalem there shall be those who escape, as the LORD has said, and among the survivors shall be those whom the LORD calls."

Reading further in Joel clearly shows that the prophet was thinking about the deliverance of the Jews from exilic bondage and the reconstruction and restoration of the city of Jerusalem (Joel 3:1–8). Yet the restoration of Israel conceived of in Acts is not about ethnic Israel and physical Jerusalem, but about a new Israel consisting of people of all races and nationalities.

After the quotation from Joel, Peter's remarks shift to a focus on Jesus of Nazareth. The description of Jesus in this speech begins with a recognition of Jesus' humanity and concludes with a declaration of Jesus as Lord and Messiah. First, Peter described Jesus as "a man," a human being much like those in Peter's audience. Second, this "man" had been "attested to you by God with deeds of power, wonders, and signs." These three descriptive words of the nature of Jesus' ministry are the most common expressions in the New Testament for the miracles of Jesus. They are words that express Jesus' works as demonstrations of divine power, as occasions of great wonder, and as indicators (signs) of the nature of Jesus' person and mission.

Yet, Peter declared that this great man of God was handed over (same word for "betrayed") to his enemies and was crucified. Peter stressed two things about the death of Jesus. First, both Jews and Gentiles were culpable in the death of Jesus. Peter said "you" put him to death, meaning the Jews (most likely Jewish leaders), with the help of "those outside the law," meaning those who do not observe the Law of Moses, i.e., Gentiles. This is likely Peter's meaning since later he mentions that "both Herod and Pontius Pilate with the Gentiles and the peoples of Israel gathered together against your holy servant Jesus" (Acts 4:27–28). Second, Peter noted that Jesus' death was "according to the definite plan and foreknowledge of God." Here one sees that in all things God is in control. And yet, while everything had happened according to God's sovereign and wise plan, that did not remove moral responsibility from those who conspired and carried out Jesus' death.

Yet, despite human effort to destroy Jesus, God overcame and defeated those evil intentions by raising Jesus from the dead. In fact, Peter stated that it was impossible for Jesus to stay in the grave because of whom Jesus was and is: the Son of God.

In Luke and Acts, the resurrection of Jesus is the heart of the Christian gospel. While Jesus' death is a critical event in the plan of God, it is described most often in Acts as the tragic unjust death of the innocent and righteous Son of God and less as an act of atonement for human sin. For Luke and Acts, the resurrection is God's ultimate validation of Jesus as Lord and Messiah and the sign of the dawning of the age of the kingdom. Because the resurrection of Jesus is so important, it is not surprising that some attention be given to the evidence for the Christian claim of Jesus' resurrection. The next part in Peter's sermon is a focus on a defense of the truthfulness of the resurrection of Jesus. Peter's argument for the resurrection of Jesus is threefold: (1) the testimony of Scripture, (2) the eyewitness testimony of the apostles, (3) and the manifestations of the Holy Spirit as evidence of the exaltation of the resurrected Jesus.

The argument from the testimony of Scripture is focused on Psalm 16:6–11, which is quoted in Acts 2:25–28, and Psalm 132:11–12, which is referred to in Acts 2:29–30. From Psalm 16:6–11, Peter argued that David, who died and was buried, prophesied that God would not let his holy one to be abandoned to the realm of the dead (literally "Hades"). Since "holy one" was interpreted to mean God's Messiah, or Jesus, it seems that the psalmist had prophesied that God would not abandon Jesus in the grave but instead raise him up. The second text, Psalm 132:11–12, states that one of David's descendants would be exalted to the throne. This psalm expresses God's promise to renew the covenant/promise that was originally given to David (2 Sam 7:10–16). That renewal of the covenant promise was fulfilled at the resurrection and exaltation of Jesus.

The second argument for Jesus' resurrection is the testimony of the apostles. In Acts, the primary work of the Twelve was to testify to the resurrection of Jesus. Based on their word, the church proclaims its message that Jesus of Nazareth is Lord and Messiah. The integrity of the gospel rests on the integrity of the apostles and their testimony.

The third argument for Jesus' resurrection is the manifestations of the Holy Spirit, specifically the phenomenon of speaking in tongues. Peter's argument is that the demonstrable outpouring of the Holy Spirit testifies to the exaltation of the living Jesus (Acts 2:33–34). This argument is supported by the citation of Psalm 110:1, "The Lord says to my Lord, 'Sit at my right hand until I make your enemies your footstool.'" Psalm 110 is an enthronement psalm for the Davidic king, and the quotation of Psalm 110:1 was for Peter an indication from Scripture that Jesus had been exalted. Peter apparently believed that God's plan was that the Holy Spirit would be given after the Son returned to the Father, or had been exalted. The visible and audible working of the Spirit was evidence that the kingdom had come upon the earth in the community of believers. The gifts demonstrate that Jesus is truly Lord as well as Messiah.

Therefore, since Scripture predicted that God would not allow his holy one to stay in the realm of the dead and experience decay, and because the apostles had actually seen the risen Jesus, and since the visible and audible manifestations of the Holy Spirit were evidence that Jesus had been not only raised but also exalted to the right hand of God, Peter concluded that this Jesus is Lord and Messiah. The dual title of Jesus here may simply be a way of emphasizing Jesus' divine nature and authority, or it may mean two separate ideas. The word "Lord" certainly conveys the idea of authority and may refer to the Gentile idea of royalty. However, this same word may also be a declaration of Jesus as divine, since in the Old Testament God is often described as Lord. The title "Messiah" (rendered "Christ" in some other translations) seems to be a reference to Jesus as the anointed one of God, the king of Israel, and the one Israelite king who had come to deliver Israel from their sin and establish the eternal kingdom of God. The tragic thing is that Peter accused his hearers of being guilty of the death of their Messiah. Upon realizing the enormity of their guilt, they cried out and asked, "What should we do?"

Peter responded with, "Repent and be baptized every one of you, in the name of Jesus Christ so that your sins may be forgiven; and you will receive the gift of the Holy Spirit" (2:38). The call for repentance and baptism was not new. Repentance often appears in the messages of the Hebrew prophets to their Israelite brothers and sisters. Baptism, most likely a ritual of immersion in water, was central to John the Baptist's message of repentance. Within Judaism there were other purification rituals involving water, and there may have been a form of baptism that was administered to Gentile converts to Judaism. The use of water was a powerful symbol for cleansing, whether for ceremonial uncleanness or moral and spiritual sin. The unique aspect of Christian baptism was that it was done "in the name of Jesus Christ" and that it was closely associated with believers' reception of the gift of the Holy Spirit. The phrase "in the name of Jesus Christ" signifies an act of faith in and submission to the authority of Jesus as the Messiah and Lord. To receive the gift of the Holy Spirit means to receive as a gift the divine Spirit that signals the beginning of the last days, or age, of God's work of salvation in the world.

According to Acts, there were a large number of people (three thousand) who responded to Peter's message with faith and submitted to baptism in the name of Jesus. For Luke, this large response was the birth of a new community of believers in Jesus—the church. Having described the beginning of the church, the author of Acts portrays the life of this primitive Christian community:

> They devoted themselves to the apostles' teaching and fellowship, to the breaking of bread and the prayers. [43] Awe came upon everyone, because many wonders and signs were being done by the apostles. [44] All who believed were together and had all things in common; [45] they would sell their possessions and goods and distribute the proceeds to all, as any had need. [46] Day by day, as they spent much time together in the temple, they broke bread at home and ate their food with glad and generous hearts, [47] praising God and having the goodwill of all the people. And day by day the Lord added to their number those who were being saved. (Acts 2:42–47)

In verse 42, the author lists four aspects of the life of this Jesus community: devotion to the apostles' teachings, fellowship, the breaking of bread, and prayer (literally, "the prayers"). It is actually possible to translate "fellowship" as "the fellowship," "the breaking of bread" as "the breaking of the bread," and "prayers" as "the prayers." In other words, these four areas may refer to specific religious activities that this Christian community was participating in. Following this list, verses 43–47 mention four activities. In summary these are:

1. The believers witnessed the miracles of the apostles' in awe and wonder.
2. They held all things in common and sold property to use the proceeds to help the poor among them.
3. They met daily together in the temple.
4. They broke bread in their homes and ate together with glad and sincere hearts.

It is possible that the second list in verses 43–47 was intended to expand on all or part of the four areas of church life summarized in verse 42. It is uncertain whether the community's witness of the wonders and signs done by the apostles is a demonstration of devotion to the apostles' teaching (2:43). However, when Acts describes these early Christians being together, holding everything in common even to the point of selling personal possessions, and giving the proceeds to those who were in need (44–45), it is likely that this was a demonstration of "devotion to fellowship." Moreover, when Acts mentions the church gathering together daily in the temple, the author was probably referring to the Jewish practice of observing the designated time of prayer. Finally, the reference to the "breaking of bread" in homes along with time of praise (2:46) is likely an expansion of the reference to a fellowship meal, which was most likely a fellowship meal that included what is commonly called the Lord's Supper, or Communion.

For Further Study

Important Names and Terms

- Pentecost
- Joel
- Glossalia (tongues)
- Dialektos (other languages/tongues)
- Repent
- Be baptized

Questions

1. What is Pentecost, and what significance did it have for Israel?
2. How is Jesus portrayed in Peter's sermon?
3. Summarize Peter's argument in support of the resurrection of Jesus.
4. In Peter's sermon, what purposes does the outpouring of the Spirit have?
5. How would you describe the nature of the first Christian community?

ACTS 3
The Healing of the Lame Man

The Healing of the Lame Man (Acts 3:1–10)

THE NEXT MAJOR NARRATIVE describes events that likely took place a few days after Pentecost. Acts describes Peter and John going to the temple at the hour of prayer, which was 3:00 p.m. The fact that these apostles were on their way to the Jerusalem temple for the hour of prayer shows that these early Jesus followers saw no contradiction between believing in Jesus as the Messiah and devoting themselves to the Jewish time of prayer, the time when sacrifices were offered in the temple. In other words, they did not cease being practicing Jews when they became disciples of Jesus. Rather, they were convinced that faith in Jesus was not only consistent with their Jewish piety but also the fulfillment of the hope of Israel.

According to the text, Peter and John encountered a lame man who was sitting and begging at the gate of the temple. Acts calls the temple gate "Beautiful" (the Beautiful Gate). Josephus describes the gate as made of "Corinthian brass" (bronze) and covered with gold and silver (*Jewish War* 5.5.201). The gate was located on the east side of the temple near both the Court of Women and the Court of the Gentiles, which would have been the outer court. Since Acts notes that people carried the lame man every day to the temple courts to beg for alms, it is clear he was a fixture known by anyone who regularly frequented this place of worship.

Though the lame man begged for alms from Peter and John, the apostles gave him something more valuable than money: a sound and healthy body. Luke records that Peter healed the man in the name of Jesus Christ. In many ways this miracle recalls the healing miracles of Jesus, i.e., the healing of the paralytic (Luke 5:17–26) and the healing of the lame man at the pool of Bethesda (John 5:1–18). Like Jesus' healings, this miracle involved no incantation or strange rituals—only an authoritative word of faith. Also, the text states that "instantly the man's feet and ankles became strong. He jumped to his feet and began to walk," a healing result much like Jesus' miracles. Yet, while Jesus healed with his own power, the apostles healed with faith in the power of Jesus.

In dramatic demonstration and celebration of his healing, the healed man went into the temple "walking, jumping, and praising God" (Acts 3:8). Luke's portrayal of the healed man's actions recalls Isaiah 35:5–6, a prophecy concerning the signs of the messianic age:

> The wilderness and the dry land shall be glad, the desert shall rejoice and blossom; like the crocus [2] it shall blossom abundantly, and rejoice with joy and singing. The glory of Lebanon shall be given to it, the majesty of Carmel and Sharon. They shall see the glory of the LORD, the majesty of our God. [3] Strengthen the weak hands, and make firm the feeble knees. [4] Say to those who are of a fearful heart, "Be strong, do not fear! Here is your God. He will come with vengeance, with terrible recompense. He will come and save you." [5] *Then the eyes of the blind shall be opened, and the ears of the deaf unstopped;* [6] *then the lame shall leap like a deer, and the tongue of the speechless sing for joy. For waters shall break forth in the wilderness, and streams in the desert.* (Isa 35:1–6, emphasis added)

Peter's Second Sermon (Acts 3:11–26)

The crowd reacted in wonder and amazement to what the apostles did and what happened to the lame man. Yet, they did not recognize or acknowledge the power of Jesus to which the apostles appealed (similar to the reaction by the residents of Lystra after the healing of a lame man in 14:8–13). According to the author, this scene occurred in the temple area called Solomon's Colonnade. Peter responded by taking the focus off John and himself and placing it on Jesus (see 14:14–15). First, Peter took no personal credit for the man's healing. Instead, Peter pointed to Jesus:

> The God of Abraham, the God of Isaac, and the God of Jacob, the God of our ancestors has glorified his servant Jesus, whom you handed over and rejected in the presence of Pilate, though he had decided to release him. [14] But you rejected the Holy and Righteous One and asked to have a murderer given to you, [15] and you killed

the Author of life, whom God raised from the dead. To this we are witnesses. (3:13–16)

With this text, Peter connected Jesus with the patriarchs of Israel (Abraham, Isaac, Jacob). The God that Jesus served is also the same God that the patriarchs served. The implication is that the religion of Jesus is not in conflict with the genuine faith of Israel. The speech reveals some important ideas concerning the nature and work of Jesus. First, Peter said God had glorified "his servant Jesus." The Greek word for "servant" (*paidea*) can also mean "child." The same word also appears in Acts 3:26, 4:27, and 30, where it is translated as "servant." In addition, the Greek Old Testament (Septuagint) translated the Hebrew word for "servant" (*ebed*) with *paidea* in Isaiah 52:13, which begins the last of the "Servant Songs" (52:13—53:12). This last song celebrates the servant of the Lord who willingly suffers unjustly for the sin of his people, a suffering that leads to the servant's death. The point is that Luke likely used *paidea* because he understood Jesus to be the Servant of the Lord mentioned in Isaiah, who would ultimately suffer and die for the sins of the people.

Peter charged his audience with handing Jesus over to the authorities to be put to death, even disowning Jesus before the Roman governor, Pilate, who had decided to release Jesus. Peter said they had "rejected the Holy and Righteous One," a possible allusion to Isaiah 53:11: "Out of his anguish he shall see light; he shall find satisfaction through his knowledge. The righteous one, my servant, shall make many righteous, and he shall bear their iniquities."

Consequently, Peter charged that they were guilty of having killed "the author of life." The Greek word *archeigos* appears four times in the New Testament (Acts 3:15; 5:31; Heb 2:10; 12:2) and can be translated as "author," "pioneer," "captain," "leader," "founder," or "originator." In the context of Acts 3, it appears that Peter is saying that Jesus is the source or originator of life, thus the translation of "author of life." How ironic it is that Peter's audience had been responsible for the killing the author of life! Nevertheless, God reversed this great injustice by raising Jesus from the dead. Again, Peter supported the claim of Jesus' resurrection by pointing to the witness of the apostles. The implication of the resurrection of Jesus is that Jesus is still alive and working. The healing of this lame man was a dramatic demonstration of the power of the living Jesus to heal, a power that one can access through faith.

Living Lord, Empowering Spirit, Testifying People

Having presented the case for Jesus as the living Son of God, Peter called his audience to faith and repentance. He said that their actions against Jesus were done in ignorance. This implies that if the people and their leaders had really known who Jesus was and is, the Messiah of Israel and Lord of all, they wouldn't have killed him. Their ignorance was rooted in their refusal to open their hearts and minds to the truth that had been revealed in Jesus. This ignorance was borne from pride and unbelief. Nevertheless, despite the moral culpability of Jesus' enemies, Jesus' death was really a fulfillment of what had been predicted by the prophets many years before. Israel had read the prophets, but misread them, which led them to misunderstand Jesus and participate in his execution. Having established both the guilt of his hearers in addition to God's mysterious plan, Peter gave them this exhortation:

> Repent therefore, and turn to God so that your sins may be wiped out, [20] so that times of refreshing may come from the presence of the Lord, and that he may send the Messiah appointed for you, that is, Jesus, [21] who must remain in heaven until the time of universal restoration that God announced long ago through his holy prophets. (Acts 3:19–21)

This double imperative ("Repent therefore, and turn to God"), followed by a promise of the wiping away of sin and ushering in times of refreshing from the Lord, is very similar to the first double imperative, in Acts 2:38, which calls for people to "Repent and be baptized in the name of Jesus Christ," followed by the promise of forgiveness of sin and the gift of the Holy Spirit. If baptism is implied in the second double imperative ("turn to God") then Peter was suggesting in this second sermon that baptism is not a work one does in order to receive God's blessing, but rather a symbolic act of turning to God in faith. And when one turns to God in faith and repentance, God will blot out the sin of that person and restore a relationship with him or her.

It is less certain what is meant by "times of refreshing." This could be another way of referring to the gift of the Holy Spirit. The Old Testament use of or allusion to "water" as a metaphor for the Spirit could make the concept of refreshment refer to the reception of the Spirit. However, Peter may be referring to the blessings of the End of the Age, when God will send the Messiah, who is Jesus, to his people. Messiah Jesus ascended into heaven to a place of exaltation, and will return at the time when God brings to fulfillment "the time of universal restoration that God announced long

The Healing of the Lame Man

ago through his holy prophets." The meaning of the restoration of all things is unclear. Some believe this has to do with the restoration of the nation of Israel. Others believe Peter was referring to the restoration of the kingdom of God, which would include people of all nations. However, it may be that restoration has to do with the renewal of the entire created order. It appears, however, that the concept of the restoration of the kingdom of God is more consistent with the theological concerns of Luke/Acts.

Peter then identified Jesus as the new prophet like Moses (Deut 18:15–19). Since Moses delivered old Israel out of slavery, led them through the wilderness to the edge of the promised land, and gave them God's law, so also Jesus delivers his people from the slavery to sin, leads them through the wilderness of this life in anticipation of the promised eternal life, and gives believers his teachings. Peter pointed out that Israel's prophets, beginning with Samuel, predicted the coming of Jesus, this Moses-like prophet, and the outpouring of the Spirit at Pentecost as the fulfillment of the hopes of Israel. The healing of the lame man would have been a sign of Jesus' prophetic ministry through the apostle. Moreover, the fact that this healed man came from the poor and outcast of society shows the prophetic vision that the Messiah will bring divine mercy, especially to the poor. Consequently, when this prophet comes, people must pay attention and listen to his words. Thus this crowd must heed the words of Jesus spoken by these apostles.

Israel was the first to receive this opportunity to experience the blessing of the Messiah due to God's promise to Abraham and his covenant with Israel. Later this blessing would be extended to Gentiles.

For Further Study

Important Names and Terms

- The Beautiful Gate
- Septuagint
- The Servant Songs
- Paidea (Greek)

Questions

1. The healing of the lame man seemed to cause some of the crowd to believe in Jesus. Why?
2. Read through Luke 22–23 and Acts 2–3. What was the significance of Jesus' death? Which passage do you find speaks most to you?
3. List the different titles given to Jesus in Acts 3.
4. Though Peter and John are apostles of Jesus, they still act very much like Jews of the day. Additionally, Peter's speech connected Jesus with the Old Testament. What were ways in which the apostles acted like Jews and portrayed Jesus as compatible with the Jewish faith?

ACTS 4

The First Arrest of Peter and John

The Arrest of Peter and John (Acts 4:1–4)

To this point the narrative of Acts has concentrated on the beginnings of the Christian movement. Beginning with chapter 4, Acts shifts focus to the challenges or obstacles that these early believers faced. Sometimes a challenge came from outside opposition to the church; other times the challenges were internal problems that threatened the very existence of the community.

Chapter 4 records that Peter and John were arrested by the temple guard and were forced to undergo interrogation by the religious authorities, i.e., the priests, the captain of the temple, and the Sadducees. The reason Luke gives for their arrest is that the authorities (namely, the Sadducees) objected to the preaching of the resurrection of Jesus. It is well documented that the Sadducees did not believe in the resurrection. Their objection to the resurrection may have its origin in their strict belief in the sole authority of the Torah (Genesis–Deuteronomy), which says nothing of resurrection, and/or their sympathies toward the Greek view of life and death, which affirmed the immortality of the soul but not the resurrection of the body. Moreover, the temple authorities may have become alarmed by the rapid growth of this new messianic community, numbering over five thousand, and the long-term implication this growth could have on Judaism as they knew it.

Peter's Defense (Acts 4:5–12)

The next morning after their arrest, Peter and John were brought before the Jewish authorities, who are described as "the rulers, elders, and scribes." Specifically mentioned in attendance are Annas (the former high priest), Caiaphas (the current high priest), John (the future high priest), and a person named Alexander, along with others. Most likely Peter and John had been called before the Sanhedrin, which functioned as something like a Jewish supreme court over both religious and civil affairs. The apostles' inquisitors asked them, "By what power or by what name did you do this?" (4:7). This question was about the source of the apostles' power to heal the lame man. Their question of the apostles' authority to heal recalls a similar question asked of Jesus following the cleansing of the temple (Luke 20:2). Peter's Spirit-filled response was in fulfillment of Jesus' promise that the Holy Spirit would teach them what to say (Matt 10:16–20; Luke 12:8–12). The author may have intended the reader to understand that Peter's response to the council was a prophetic utterance since he said the apostle was "filled with the Holy Spirit."

Peter noted that the council had asked about how the lame man was healed (literally, "has been healed"), which he also described as "a good deed." The Greek word for "healed" (*sozo*) is the normal word for "save." Later in verse 12 Peter said, "There is salvation in no one else, for there is no other name under heaven given among mortals by which we must be *saved*." For Peter to claim that one can only be saved through this name means that Jesus is the source and power of both physical and spiritual healing. Peter then returned to the core belief of the early disciples: "This man is standing before you in good health by the name of Jesus Christ of Nazareth, whom you crucified, whom God raised from the dead" (4:10b). The opponents of Jesus had tried to rid themselves of him and, as Jesus hung on the cross, it appeared as if they had succeeded. But humans can never thwart the plans of God for humankind and the world. God turned the Sanhedrin's apparent victory into defeat by raising Jesus from the dead. It was through the living Jesus that Peter claimed the lame man was healed. Not only was Jesus the source of the lame man's healing; he was the one through whom God brought salvation to the world. Jesus was also the promised Messiah of Israel, the one for whom Israel had been looking and praying. Drawing from the Psalms, Peter said "This Jesus is 'the stone that was rejected by you, the builders; it has become the cornerstone'" (4:11). The quotation comes from Psalm 118:

> The stone that the builders rejected
> has become the chief cornerstone.
> ²³ This is the LORD's doing;
> it is marvelous in our eyes.
> ²⁴ This is the day that the LORD has made;
> let us rejoice and be glad in it.
> ²⁵ Save us, we beseech you, O LORD!
> O LORD, we beseech you, give us success!
> ²⁶ Blessed is the one who comes in the name of the LORD.
> We bless you from the house of the LORD. ²⁷
> The LORD is God,
> and he has given us light.
> Bind the festal procession with branches,
> up to the horns of the altar. (Ps 118:22–27)

This text refers to Israel, who, after the destruction of Jerusalem and the temple and also the deportation of her people, was regarded as weak and insignificant by the nations. Yet Israel continued to hope that one day God would vindicate and exalt his people. Thus the rejected stone becomes the cornerstone, the stone that is the foundation for the building of any structure. However, Peter adapted this psalm to refer to Jesus instead of Israel. The apostle also modified the quotation to make it also apply to the religious leaders. The Hebrew wording in Psalm 118:22, "The stone that the builders rejected," is changed in Luke's Greek translation to "the stone that was rejected by *you*, the builders." Thus this Jesus whom these religious leaders had rejected and participated in his death is now in the position of power and authority. Moreover, Jesus is not only the vindicated prophet who had suffered an unjust death and whom God raised from the dead; he is the true source of salvation, the way to an authentic relationship with God.

The Verdict of the Trial (Acts 4:13–22)

After Peter said this, Acts notes that the leaders recognized that Peter and John had been with Jesus. Even though it was clear the apostles were uneducated (literally, "illiterate") men and, like Jesus, had not been formally trained by a rabbi, they demonstrated, as Jesus had, a boldness and possibly prophetic zeal.

The council could not deny that the man had been healed. Yet they were concerned that the message about Jesus would spread throughout the community and beyond. And since the heart of the apostle's message was the death and resurrection of Jesus, the council ordered Peter and John to no longer speak or preach in the name of Jesus. The council would accept the miracle of the lame man as real but denied that he was healed by the name and power of Jesus.

Peter and John responded to the council's orders by stating that the council must do what it believes is right. Nevertheless, Peter and John must continue to speak about what they have seen and heard. A literal translation of 4:20 reads: "For we are not able to speak except what we have seen and heard." Without sufficient evidence to punish them and with pressure from the crowd, who were still excited over the healing of the lame man, the council decided to release the apostles with a warning not to preach in the name of Jesus. This amounted to something like a slap on the wrist.

The Prayer of the Jerusalem Church (4:23–31)

After Peter and John were released, they returned to their fellow believers and told them what had happened. During what may have been a gathering for worship, a prayer was offered by the church. Luke is clear that the entire gathered community of believers participated in this prayer:

> "Sovereign Lord, who made the heaven and the earth, the sea, and everything in them, [25] it is you who said by the Holy Spirit through our ancestor David, your servant:
>
> 'Why did the Gentiles rage, and the peoples imagine vain things? [26] The kings of the earth took their stand, and the rulers have gathered together against the Lord and against his Messiah.'
>
> [27] For in this city, in fact, both Herod and Pontius Pilate, with the Gentiles and the peoples of Israel, gathered together against your holy servant Jesus, whom you anointed, [28] to do whatever your hand and your plan had predestined to take place. [29] And now, Lord, look at their threats, and grant to your servants to speak your word with all boldness, [30] while you stretch out your hand to heal, and signs and wonders are performed through the name of your holy servant Jesus." (4:24b–30)

The prayer opens with an acknowledgement of the sovereign power of God, the creator of all things (note similar expressions in Acts 14:15 and 17:24). This opening address to God expresses the source of the early church's courage. The implication of these words is that evil is powerless before the sovereign God and that neither persecution nor the threat of

The First Arrest of Peter and John

persecution can thwart the purpose and will of God. Over and over again, Acts shows that the early Christians faced difficulties of various kinds and yet were able to overcome them. To emphasize their confidence in God, this primitive Jesus community cited from Psalm 2. The psalm is introduced with an affirmation that God spoke "by the Holy Spirit through our ancestor David, your servant David":

> [1] Why do the nations conspire,
> and the peoples plot in vain?
> [2] The kings of the earth set themselves,
> and the rulers take counsel together,
> against the LORD
> and his anointed. (Ps 2:1–2)

Psalm 2 originally was a royal or coronation psalm. It was written to give honor to the new king of Israel. It reaffirms the role of the king as God's representative or son. The theological origins of this psalm go back to 1 Samuel 7:5–16, which records the covenant God established with David and his descendants, securing the house of David as the royal line of Israel. However, it is clear that the early church applied Psalm 2 to Jesus. This is even more clear in Paul's quotation of Psalm 2:7 in Acts 13:33: "You are my son; today I have become your father" (NIV). The saying also appears in the baptismal and transfiguration narratives of the gospels (Matt 4:17; 17:5; Mark 1:11; 9:7; Luke 3:22; 9:35). Based on this quotation, this prayer affirmed two things: first, there have and always will be enemies against God and his servants, in this case God's "anointed" ("Messiah" means "anointed one"), the king; second, the enemies of God are fundamentally powerless before God. While God and his people have always had to face opposition, the power of these opponents is nothing compared to God and they cannot stop or alter his plan. For the writer of Acts, Herod, Pilate, other Gentiles, and the unbelievers in Israel all stood in opposition to Jesus just as the psalmist described. Yet their rejection and opposition to the Messiah of Israel was actually part of God's plan.

Thus, when one recognizes that God is the sovereign creator of the universe, he/she also realizes that opposition, threats, and persecution are only the enemies' vain attempt to defeat God—an attempt doomed to failure. From this perspective, prayer takes on a different dynamic and purpose. This prayer concludes with specific requests of God by these disciples:

> And now, Lord, look at their threats, and grant to your servants to
> speak your word with all boldness, [30] while you stretch out your

> hand to heal, and signs and wonders are performed through the
> name of your holy servant Jesus. (4:29–30)

Instead of praying for deliverance, protection, or no persecution, the early disciples prayed for boldness of speech with accompanying miraculous signs. Instead of protection and retreat, they prayed that God would use their mouths and hands to witness to the living Jesus, who is Lord and Messiah. The source of their boldness rested in their trust in the power of God. Despite these threats, they were convinced that the enemies would not endure. Instead, they believed that through faith in Jesus the church would be triumphant.

The results of their prayer were dramatic. Luke says that "the place in which they were gathered together was shaken" (4:31). Shaking ground is sometimes an indication of the presence of God (Exod 19:18; Isa 6:4). The text also states that "they were all filled with the Holy Spirit" (4:31). These early Christians had prayed for boldness and divine empowerment to witness for Jesus, and God had answered their prayer.

Life in the Early Church: A Community Moved by the Spirit (Acts 4:32–37)

What does a Spirit-filled Jesus community look like? How do they live? Acts 4:32–37 presents a brief portrait of early church life. One purpose for this description is to show that the Spirit-directed Jesus community promoted peaceful and healthy community life. Acts states that the believers were "of one heart and soul" (4:32). This description is a common Greek expression for friendship. Thus, from at least a Hellenistic perspective, these early Christians had become a network of close friends. The text says that they held everything in common, the same description of the church found in Acts 2:44. Similarly, the Greek's view of friendship often included having all things in common. To further highlight the shared life of these early Christians, Acts states, "There was not a needy person among them" (4:34). Perhaps more than the Greek idea of friendship, or even the theory of communism, is the likelihood that Luke is alluding to the instructions concerning the Sabbatical year (Deut 15:1–18) or Jubilee (Lev 25:8–17). This is consistent with Jesus' view of his ministry in Luke 4:18–19, where Jesus quoted mostly from Isaiah 61, a text that had become associated with Jubilee.

Representing this Spirit-filled community of friends, who shared their life together, were the apostles, who testified to the resurrection with great power, most likely with and through miraculous works. Consequently, the early Jerusalem church had begun to fulfill its mission. Luke's example of a person who lived this two-fold mission of the church is Barnabas. The name "Barnabas," which means "son of encouragement," was a nickname that apparently had been given to a certain Levite named Joseph, whom Acts said was a native of the island of Cypress. As a Levite, Barnabas belonged to the priestly tribe of Israel, but since he grew up on Cypress, Barnabas would have been more comfortable in the Gentile world than most of his traditional Jewish brothers. The text indicates that Barnabas owned some land, which he sold, giving the proceeds to the apostles to be used to help the poor. According to Torah, priests were not to own property, although most Levites likely did. In addition to portraying Barnabas as a generous man who gave most of what he owned to help others, the text also probably implies that the selling of the land was an act of repentance.

For Further Study

Important Names and Terms

- Sadducee
- Caiaphas
- Barnabas
- Jubilee

Questions

1. What is meant by a "cornerstone"?
2. Why did the Jewish council strongly prohibit the preaching of the gospel? Was there something in its message that particularly troubled the Jewish leadership?
3. What can be learned about the Christian view of the sovereignty of God from Acts 4?
4. Based on Acts 2 and 4, what was the primitive church's understanding of wealth?

ACTS 5

Ananias and Sapphira

Ananias and Sapphira (Acts 5:1–11)

Luke described the life of the early Spirit-filled Christian community as bold, evangelistic, unselfish, and compassionate. He included Barnabas as a clear example of this community. Underlying Luke's summary are the qualities of genuineness and sincerity. The story of Ananias and Sapphira is set in stark contrast to the description of both the early church (4:32–35) in general and Barnabas (4:36–37) in particular. This narrative marks the second time that the early church faced a threat to its existence. Yet this threat comes from within the community itself, from members who were exposed as hypocrites.

Some interpreters have suggested that this story is reminiscent of the story of Achan in Joshua 7. According to Joshua 7, following the dramatic victory over the fortified city of Jericho, the Israelites suffered an unexpected and humiliating defeat at the little outpost of Ai, which resulted in the death of about thirty-six men. The Lord informed Joshua that the cause of Israel's defeat was the sin of Achan, who had taken forbidden spoils of war out of Jericho. His sin had removed God's veil of protection from Israel. The crisis was resolved with the execution of Achan and his family. In the case of Ananias and Sapphira, their sin does not appear to be direct disobedience, but hypocrisy. They had sold some land and gave part of the proceeds of the sale to the apostles, but claimed they were giving all the proceeds. Acts does not indicate what the judgment might have been for someone who openly gave only part of his possessions. Moreover, it seems each member was free to decide how they would use their personal resources (5:4–5). Peter through the Holy Spirit knew immediately that Ananias had lied. His condemnation of Ananias shows that the apostle did not regard him as a genuine follower of Jesus. He said that Satan had filled their (Ananias and Sapphira) hearts (5:3), in contrast to the church, which had been filled with the Holy Spirit (4:31). If the church had been moved by the Spirit to care for the poor, then Ananias and Sapphira's self-serving acts were attempts to manipulate and deceive the Spirit, thereby manipulating and deceiving the church. Perhaps they had pretended to be of one heart and mind with the other believers. Furthermore, Peter accused them of lying to the Holy Spirit (5:3) and to God (5:4). Peter later told Sapphira that she and her husband had put the Spirit of the Lord to the test (5:9).

After Ananias and Sapphira were separately confronted with their hypocrisy, they each fell down and immediately died. The author is not interested in the physical cause of death; the description would seem to suggest heart attack or stroke. Nowhere does it say that Peter struck them dead or order others to put them to death. If that is what happened, then Luke has rewritten the story to remove any human involvement in these deaths. While not explicitly stated, Luke is likely implying that their deaths were caused by God. The church reacted to their deaths with "great fear." These deaths were an indication for everyone that Christian discipleship requires serious personal responsibility, and hypocrisy and dishonesty cannot be tolerated. Moreover, as the sin of Achan prevented Israel from moving forward in their conquest of Canaan, so also hypocrisy and dishonesty had made it more difficult for the church to carry out its mission.

The Greek word for "church" (*ekklesia*) appears first in Acts in 5:11. While this may be merely a stylistic feature of Acts, it is also possible that Luke is being theologically deliberate with this choice of word. *Ekklesia* appears in the Greek Old Testament (Septuagint) as a translation of the Hebrew *qahal*, a common word for the congregation of Israel. By using *ekklesia* here, Luke is connecting the early Christian community with the covenant community of God of the Old Testament, especially as they faced the challenge of sin within the community, as in the case of Achan.

Fear and Attraction (Acts 5:12–16)

The impact of these deaths spread beyond the church. In response to this, Luke says that "None of the rest dared to join them" (5:13), and this was the case for a short while, even though the people were amazed and attracted to this believing community. The text indicates that "many signs and wonders were done among the people through the apostles" (5:12), which suggests that the dramatic removal of sin from the Christian camp had an empowering effect. Despite the mixture of fear and attraction, the church experienced significant numerical growth with conversions of men and women to Jesus. Moreover, the healing ministry of Peter powerfully expanded to take on large numbers. Crowds flock to Peter to be healed—even by his shadow—reminiscent of Jesus' healings (Luke 8:40–55).

Second Arrest and Imprisonment (Acts 5:17–26)

The increased popularity of the apostles, coupled with their defiance of the prohibition to preach in the name of Jesus, provoked the Jewish religious authorities, especially the Sadducees, to have Peter and John arrested again and put into jail. The first time Peter and John were arrested the Sanhedrin merely gave them a warning along with a prohibition against preaching. At that time, the enthusiasm of the crowd may have caused the council to back down. When they arrested the apostles a second time, Luke quickly tells us that the apostles were miraculously delivered by an angel, who instructed them to return to the temple and preach about the Christian life (literally, "this life"; see 3:14; 13:26). After two arrests, the religious leaders had been unsuccessful in silencing the preaching of the gospel. In fact, Luke somewhat humorously portrays the prison guards futilely looking for their prisoners who were missing. When it was learned that their prisoners were in the temple preaching, the Sanhedrin ordered that they quietly arrest the apostles and bring them back to prison.

Third Imprisonment and Second Hearing before the High Priest (5:27–32)

After their third arrest, the apostles were brought before the Sanhedrin. The high priest began by reminding the apostles of their previous orders not to preach Jesus. The Sanhedrin expressed their strong dislike for being charged with Jesus' death. Peter responded by saying, "We must obey God rather than any human authority" (5:29). This is the first indication that Christians may have to choose between their loyalty to civil authority and loyalty to God. After that, Peter summarized the events of Jesus' death and resurrection. In shocking language Peter accused them of killing Jesus "by hanging him on a tree" (Acts 5:30; see Deut 21:22–23). The importance of stressing Jesus' death as a hanging is to point out that the action of crucifixion or hanging actually brought a curse upon him. Through crucifixion, Jesus' opponents held him in contempt. Yet, in contrast to the curse, God exalted (showed high honor to) Jesus by resurrecting him, raising him to right hand, and making him "Leader and Savior" (Acts 5:31), which may suggest he is the Messiah.

The Intercession of Gamaliel (Acts 5:33–42)

The message of Peter so infuriated the Sadducees that they wanted to kill both Peter and John. Yet, they likely needed support from at least some of the Pharisees in order to carry out their plan. At this point in the story, the apostles found deliverance from an unlikely source, Gamaliel. This is probably Gamaliel the elder, the leading rabbi of the rabbinical school of Hillel. He is described as a Pharisee, whom Paul later described as his former teacher and mentor. In this story, Gamaliel interceded for the apostles and prevented an act of violence which saved their lives.

Gamaliel's argument seems based on the pharisaic faith in the providence of God. Pharisees believed God was in control of everything and worked out events in history to accomplish his purposes. He advised the authorities to let Peter and John go and let God deal with them (likely through the Roman government) by either blessing their work or disposing of them as frauds. As examples, Gamaliel referred to two previous failed messianic or revolutionary movements. He mentioned a certain Theudas, who led four hunrdred men in a failed attempt to carry out a messianic revolt. Josephus also mentions a Theudas (*Antiquities of the Jews*, 20.98), who was a revolutionary leader, but this Theudas lived and died around A.D. 44. So, either Gamaliel was referring to another Theudas who appeared much earlier, or Luke has inserted into the mouth of Gamaliel this reference to a later person. The second failed rebel was Judas. This was probably Judas the Galilean, the probable founder of the Zealots, mentioned by Josephus as being opposed to the levying of taxes by the Romans (*Antiquities of the Jews*, 18.4.23). The point of Gamaliel's argument is that other self-proclaimed Messiahs came and went along with their followers, but they didn't succeed because God was opposed to what they were doing. Similarly, he suggests that if the Jesus movement fails, which he likely expected, it will happen because God did not bless it with success. However, if the Jesus movement succeeds, then perhaps God is behind it. Possibly, Gamaliel wanted to prevent a situation that could cause unrest and bring the wrath of the Roman Empire upon them. Fortunately for the church, Gamaliel's advice was accepted. After having the apostles flogged, the officials ordered them not to preach in the name of Jesus, an order they immediately ignored. Instead, Luke states they rejoiced to have been considered worthy to suffer for Jesus and continued to teach and preach Jesus as the Christ.

It is worth noting that while Gamaliel most likely believed the Christian movement would fail, his very words, for Luke, became an endorsement of the validity of this new faith. Though small in number and resources, the followers of Jesus faced every challenged with boldness and courage, unwilling to compromise their commitment to the one they believed to be Messiah. Moreover, Acts shows that no matter the challenge or threat, God led the church through it triumphantly. God's will for the church and the world cannot be changed or stopped.

For Further Study

Important Names and Terms

- Ananias
- Sapphira
- Gamaliel
- Theudas
- Judas the Galilean
- Josephus
- Qahal
- Achan

Questions

1. Why is hypocrisy treated so harshly in Acts 5?
2. According to Acts, how should disciples of Jesus regard and use their financial resources?
3. Does Acts describe God as active in the life and ministry of the church?
4. How does Acts regard challenges and threats to the church?

ACTS 6

The Selection of the Seven to Care for Widows

The Choosing of the Seven to Care for the Widows (Acts 6:1–7)

Having overcome the threat of persecution of death, Luke shifts focus to describe other challenges this young church faced, namely internal division and complaints. Ironically, this problem was partly the result of the rapid growth of the church, which placed considerable strain on the current organizational structure. Complaints arose among the Hellenistic Jews concerning the care of their widows. The word "widow" referred not only to women who had lost their husbands to death but also, symbolically, to the poor. Even today, the majority of the poor in any country are women. Interestingly, the Greek word for "complained" (*goggusmos*) was used in the Septuagint to refer to the murmuring or complaining of Israel in the wilderness. Thus, as Israel under Moses often complained when there was lack of food or water, this early church—the new Israel—complained to the apostles concerning a problem of food distribution.

One difference between the complaining of Israel and that of the church is the latter was associated with a significant cultural divide between the Hellenistic Jews and the Hebrews within the church. The Hellenistic Jews were Greek-speaking Jewish Christians probably originating from outside of Palestine, while the Hebrews were Palestinian Jewish Christians. An imperfect modern-day comparison might be the difference between a native-born Italian, who primarily speaks Italian and dresses and eats only things Italian, and a second or third-generation Italian American, who has become fully a part of American culture. It is likely that Hebraic Jews believed the Hellenistic Jews had taken on too much on the cultural traits of the Gentile world. The tension between these two groups became dangerously apparent when Hellenistic Jews complained that their widows were being neglected while the widows of the Hebraic Jews were being cared for. This was a charge of discrimination partly rooted in a clash of cultures.

From the beginning of the church, it appears that the apostles oversaw the care of the needy as well as the preaching of the gospel. As long as the needy were a relatively small group, this was manageable. However, the rapid growth of the church in Jerusalem made it impossible for the apostles to personally supervise the food distribution program, which left the people in the community to fend for themselves. Most likely the Hebraic Jews outnumbered the Hellenistic Jews and thus controlled the food distribution. The apostles' solution to this focused on getting food to those who needed it. Since the apostles understood that God had called them to the ministry of the word and to prayer, and that managing charitable distributions would impinge upon these duties, they recommended for the church to select seven men to oversee the distribution. To guide the church in the selection process, the apostles set forth some qualifications for the men to be selected for this ministry. These men were to be people of good reputation, full of the Spirit and of wisdom. Based on these criteria, the church selected seven men, whom the apostles then prayed for and laid their hands on, a sign of a divine commission and equipment. The names of the seven chosen by the church were Stephen, Philip, Prochorus, Nicanor, Timon, Parmenas, and Nicolaus, a proselyte of Antioch. Nicolaus is called a proselyte, which probably means he was a Gentile who had converted to Judaism before becoming a believer in Jesus. With the exception of Stephen and Philip, little if anything is known about these men selected to oversee the distribution of food to widows.

Traditionally, this text has been interpreted to narrate the establishment of the first deacons of the church. However, were these seven men the first deacons? Not only does this interpretation assume that Luke intended to write about the establishment of a church office of deacon, it also assumes that the work of a deacon has to do with the physical and monetary resources of the church. The Greek word translated "deacon" is *diakonos*, which can mean "servant," "minister," or "deacon." The related verb, *diakoneo*, means "to serve," and the related noun *diakonia* means "service" or "ministry." *Diakoneo* appears in 6:2 and is translated "wait on tables," and *diakonia* appears in 6:1 and is translated as "daily distribution."

The Selection of the Seven to Care for Widows

Additionally, *diakonia* appears again in 6:4 as "serving." *Diakonos*, though, does not appear in Acts 6, so from a purely linguistic perspective the seven men are never called "deacons." Nevertheless, it is clear that their jobs involved service, and actually the responsibility of the seven in Acts is similar to what is said earlier of the apostles (4:47) and later of the elders (11:30). While it is going too far to call these seven men deacons, they may have been the forerunners of either deacons or elders, or they simply may have been special servants of the church.

Luke narrates that the early church faced a difficult internal organizational problem and resolved it peaceably. The problem allowed for two cultural groups within the church to work together, and the solution was found in reshaping the leadership by delegating the responsibility of caring for the poor. Thus another challenge, this time internal, was successfully addressed. Yet the function of this story is larger than the solution of an organizational nightmare or that another problem was overcome. The story introduces the reader to Stephen and Philip, whose ministry beyond the care of widows had a profound and lasting impact on the church. That impact, however, would involve more persecution, suffering, and death.

The Arrest and Trial of Stephen (Acts 6:8–15)

The author describes Stephen as "full of grace and power" (6:8). The term "power" probably refers to the miracles performed by Stephen, and "grace" points to the blessings resulting from the miracles or gracious power. The qualities of power and grace are usually associated with the apostles (4:33). Thus, Luke favorably compares the ministry of Stephen to that of the apostles. To further highlight the miraculous works associated with Stephen's ministry, Luke states that Stephen "did great wonders and signs among the people" (6:8). In other words, Stephen's ministry was like that of a prophet who had been filled with the Spirit (2:19, 22, 43, 4:16; 5:12).

Not only was Stephen able to perform great miracles in the name of Jesus, he also could effectively argue the case for Jesus as Messiah before Jews in the synagogue. During his earthly ministry, Jesus had promised the Holy Spirit and wisdom to his disciples when they were called on to defend their faith in Jesus (Luke 12:12; 21:15). Stephen's proclamation and defense of the gospel showed that same wisdom and Spirit. Most likely, Stephen's interpretation of the OT showed how the Scriptures looked forward to the coming of Christ, which was evidence of this wisdom from the Spirit.

Luke mentions that Stephen often spoke in the Synagogue of the Freedmen, a gathering place for ex-slaves and Jews from the Diaspora. Perhaps Stephen believed his own Hellenistic background gave him an opportunity to connect with these people for the gospel. But unfortunately, his strategy only resulted in being charged as a traitor to his own people and traditional religion. Stephen was arrested and brought before the Sanhedrin to face charges of blasphemy. The charges are expressed in different ways throughout this text:

> "We have heard him speak blasphemous words against Moses and God." (6:11b)

> "This man never stops saying things against this holy place and the law; [14] for we have heard him say that this Jesus of Nazareth will destroy this place and will change the customs that Moses handed on to us." (6:13b–14)

The charges of the accusers appear to have been false or exaggerated and the result of a conspiracy—similar to the ones brought against Jesus. While it is true that Jesus prophesied the destruction of the temple as a divine judgment on the sinfulness and unbelief of Israel (Luke 21:5–24), the charge that Stephen claimed Jesus would destroy the temple is clearly twisted (Matt 26:61, 27:40; Mark 14:58, 15:29; John 2:19–21). Yet Stephen's words from Jesus were not merely the words of some misguided radical self-proclaimed prophet. On the contrary, these words were interpreted by the authorities as an all-out attack on Jewish faith and tradition. The customs from Moses that Jesus would change probably refer to cultic and dietary regulations, which Jesus had said were no longer applicable for believers. As for the temple, his enemies understood him to be talking about something more than divine destruction on the Last Day. Rather, they believed he was advocating the abolishment of the traditional cultic ceremonies and purity codes. Thus, Stephen was charged with being against the temple and its cultic practices. Of course, without the temple and the cultic and purity regulations, Judaism would have been profoundly changed. To a large measure, then, Stephen's opponents saw him as someone who had rejected traditional Judaism. The text notes that when Stephen was arrested and brought before the Sanhedrin, the people saw that Stephen's face was like that of an angel. Since angels are often described as having glowing faces, it may be that Stephen's face was reminiscent of Moses' face, which glowed after coming down from the mountain.

The Selection of the Seven to Care for Widows

For Further Study

Important Names and Terms

- The Hellenists
- The Hebrews
- Diakonos
- Proselyte
- Nicolaus

Questions

1. Do cultural differences still provoke friction and division in the church?
2. What happened that prevented the apostles from overseeing the distribution of food?
3. Concerning church leadership and ministry, what can be learned from the story about the choosing of the seven to oversee the distribution?
4. Stephen was accused in part of rejecting traditional Jewish forms of worship and piety. How important are the forms of worship and piety?

ACTS 7:1—8:3

The Speech of Stephen

General Introduction

AFTER CHARGES OF BLASPHEMY had been brought against him, Stephen responded with what has been called his defense. While this speech does address the charges against him, it is hardly a simple defense speech. Instead, the speech is more like a prophetic sermon designed to expose the unfaithfulness of the Jewish religious leaders. From a stylistic perspective, this speech is a review of the history of Israel beginning with the call of Abraham. The purpose of this review is to point out errors in the thinking of the Jewish leadership and to charge them with sin. The basic themes of this speech are as follows:

1. God has always been present with his people and not confined to a specific location, such as the temple.
2. Israel's history is one of rejection and disobedience to those whom God had sent.
3. The temple and the Law cannot protect Israel from the consequences of their sin.

The Presence of God with His People

In his speech, God is described as one who acts. In fact, God is the main actor of the entire speech. God appears (7: 3), speaks (7:3, 6), moves (7:4), gives an inheritance (7:5), promises (7:7), judges (7:7), and gives a covenant (7:8). The speech opens with Stephen declaring that God had appeared to

The Speech of Stephen

Abraham and called him to leave his homeland and go to a new land he would show him. God established a covenant with Abraham, and as part of that covenant God promised that he would give Abraham this promised land, which—as indicated in Genesis—would be the place where a great nation would be formed from his descendants. Also, God told him that his people would experience a long period of hardship and slavery but that God would eventually rescue them.

Among the descendants of Abraham would come the twelve sons of Jacob, often known as the twelve patriarchs. Yet, even among those who formed that foundation of the nation of Israel, there was envy and hatred against Joseph, one of their brothers. So great was their hatred against him that they sold him into slavery in Egypt. Nevertheless, the Scriptures assure that the Lord was with Joseph. Through slavery, false charges, and imprisonment, God rescued Joseph from all these troubles and made him ruler over Egypt, second only to Pharaoh. Thus, even in a distant land and in very dire circumstances, God was near Joseph because he trusted and followed him.

In a similar way, God, through an angel, appeared to Moses in the desert at the burning bush and sent him to Egypt to bring his people out of bondage. Then, through Moses, God led Israel into the wilderness to Mt. Sinai, where they worshipped him. Israel's worship included the tent of witness, in which in God dwelt with his people and led them into the promised land.

Yet, if God dwelt with his people by means of a lowly tent, why was it necessary for Solomon to build the temple? After all, even Solomon said that God does not dwell in a house made with hands. Curiously, Stephen said that the tent of meeting was built in accordance with a specific pattern from God but that the temple was made with human hands. Some scholars contend that the natural way to interpret this is that God specifically commanded and gave instruction concerning the building and design of this sacred tent, but said nothing about a temple. In other words, the temple was a human innovation and modification to God's plan. The clear implication of this interpretation is that Stephen was expressing anti-temple views. Other scholars suggest that Stephen's speech is not anti-temple but rather a condemnation of an overreliance on the temple, which resulted in a virtual deification of the sanctuary. The danger of this view is that it restricts and limits one's conception of God. The Solomon quotation served to remind Stephen's audience that while a temple may have its place, it does not and cannot limit or contain God. The subtle implication of Stephen's line of argument is that God cannot be limited to any geographical locale, people, or nationality.

The History of Rejection and Disobedience

The second major point stressed in this speech is that Israel has a history of mistreating and rejecting those who would later be their leaders. Two examples of rejection are mentioned: Joseph and Moses. The speech recalls the story in Genesis when Joseph's brothers sold him into slavery. Prior to their mistreatment, Joseph had been the favored son of Jacob, who treated him with special honor. Then Joseph's dreams of future glory and honor served to provoke his brothers to abuse Joseph by selling him into slavery. Yet, Stephen noted, God honored Joseph's faithfulness by delivering him through slavery, slander, and false imprisonment to attain a position of power and honor in Egypt. Later when the famine threatened to destroy his family, not only did Joseph reveal himself to his brothers, he also helped them and their families to survive the famine.

The other example of rejection is in the story of Moses. Stephen's retelling of the story begins with a review of Moses' early years, stating how he was raised by the daughter of Pharaoh even though he was born an Israelite. Moreover, Stephen pointed out that this young man of privilege and power had sympathy for the desperate condition of his people and demonstrated his concern when he rescued an Israelite who was being beaten by an Egyptian. Moses not only defended his fellow Israelite but killed a cruel and violent Egyptian taskmaster. Yet the Israelites were not grateful for what he had done and even rejected him as their leader and deliverer. With no support from the Israelites and with the blood of an Egyptian on his hands, Moses was forced to flee into the wilderness to escape Pharaoh's wrath. While in the desert, God revealed himself to Moses and sent him back to deliver Israel from Egypt. Nevertheless, Israel initially refused to follow Moses and accept his authority—the very one God raised up to be a prophet. This stubborn and disobedient tendency of Israel is further evident in the numerous instances of idolatry along with the making of images, such as the golden calf in the desert. Stephen quoted from Amos to stress the ongoing problem of idolatry, which ultimately led to the exile (7:43).

The figures of Joseph and Moses serve as precursors to Jesus, the one who was rejected by his own people and yet through whom these same people could find deliverance. Thus the actions of the Jews regarding Jesus and his people were consistent with what their ancestors had done to men God had sent to deliver them.

The Temple and Law Cannot Protect against Wickedness

Having reviewed the history of Israel, Stephen concluded by charging his audience with following in their ancestor's footsteps. He accused them of resisting the Holy Spirit, persecuting the prophets like their ancestors, and failing to keep the Law. It was not Stephen who stood under divine judgment, but his accusers, who hid behind their positions of authority and respect and observed the ritualistic requirements of the Law, including temple worship. Yet, their rejection of Jesus and mistreatment of his people showed their own disobedience to the Law.

The Stoning of Stephen (7:54–60; 8:1–3)

The response of the Sanhedrin was swift and furious. Stephen had just accused them of unfaithfulness to God and his Law. While the text is unclear, it is reasonable to assume that the fury of the Sanhedrin was about to explode with a call to expel and physically punish this preacher. But the punishment escalated into an execution by stoning. The stoning was provoked when Stephen said he saw Jesus standing beside the throne of God, which meant that Jesus was on equal footing with God. It was one thing to accuse the Sanhedrin of disobeying the Law, but it was quite another to claim that Jesus had been exalted to the right hand of the throne of God. That was blasphemy according to their thinking and required harsh punishment. Actually, the stoning of Stephen was not a formal execution authorized by the Sanhedrin, for only Rome had the right to formally execute someone. Rather, it was the result of a mob riot, which the temple authorities undoubtedly supported.

Luke tells the story of Stephen's death in light of the death of Jesus. He did this by including Stephen's dying words, "Lord, do not hold this sin against them" (7:60), which is very similar to the words of Jesus' prayer on the cross, "Father, forgive them, for they do not know what they are doing" (Luke 23:34). Also, Stephen prayed, "Lord Jesus, receive my spirit" (7:59), similar to Jesus' prayer, "Father, into your hands I commend my spirit" (Luke 23:46). The point is that Stephen's death was Christ-like. The story of Stephen ends here with his death, but his influence would continue throughout Luke's narrative. The text notes that a young man, Saul, held the garments of Stephen's executioners and would soon take the lead in a general persecution of Christians. Yet this Saul, later known as Paul, became the next lightning rod and trailblazer for this fledgling Jesus movement.

For Further Study

Important Names and Terms

- Haran
- Rephan
- Moloch
- Midian

Questions

1. Stephen may have been criticizing the leaders of confining and limiting God in a physical place, the temple. Do people today sometimes confine or limit God? How?

2. Stephen may have been suggesting that the rejection of Jesus was consistent with Israel's previous rejection of Joseph and Moses. In light of this, how is Jesus like Joseph and Moses?

3. Read Jeremiah 7:1–15. How was Stephen's attitude towards the temple similar to Jeremiah's? How was Stephen's overall speech similar to the prophet's sermon?

ACTS 8:4—12:25

The First Persecution and Expansion of the Church

ACTS 8:4–40

The Ministry of Philip

Introduction

FOLLOWING THE DEATH OF Stephen, a general persecution arose against the church. This caused many Christians to flee Jerusalem and scatter to different locations. After Luke describes the persecution led by Saul, a series of events are narrated that profoundly changed the nature and culture of the Christian movement. The events are as follows:

1. Philip evangelizes in Samaria (8:4–25).
2. Philip evangelizes the Ethiopian eunuch (8:26–40).
3. Saul becomes a believer in Jesus and a preacher of the gospel (9:1–31).
4. Peter ministers in Lydda and Joppa (9:32–43).
5. Cornelius the Roman Centurion becomes a believer in Jesus (10:1–48).
6. Peter defends his evangelizing of the Gentile Cornelius and family (11:1–18).
7. The Antioch church is established (11:19–26).

These stories show the gradual expansion of the boundaries of the church to people of all cultures and backgrounds. After the interlude in chapter 12, in which Luke narrates the threats to the church by Herod Agrippa, who had the apostle James executed and Peter imprisoned, the story then shifts to the spread of the gospel throughout the world by the mission journeys and ministry of Paul (chs. 13–21). Acts 8–11 narrates the transitional stage of the church, moving from its exclusive Jewish roots to a more international and intercultural movement of disciples of Jesus.

The stories appear in Acts as if they took place in sequential order: (1) the evangelism of the those on the margins of Judaism, 8: 4–40; (2) the conversion of the lead persecutor of Christians, 9:1–31; (3) the ministry of Peter beyond the confines of Jerusalem and Judea, 9:32–43; the conversion of the first Gentile, 10:1—11:18; and the establishment of the first racially integrated church, 11:19–26. However, it may be that Luke intended his readers to understand that the persecution sparked the scattering of Christians, which led to a number of things taking place independently, indicating a religious movement in dynamic transition. Nevertheless, we will discuss these stories in the order in which they appear in Acts.

Preaching in Samaria and the conversion of Simon the Sorcerer (8:1–25)

The Samaritans

The first event following the scattering of the church was the evangelism of the Samaritans by Philip. According to 2 Kings 17:24–34, the Samaritans were the descendants of the intermarriages of Jews who had not been sent away into exile and people of other nations. The text indicates that an Israelite priest taught them the faith of Moses and how to worship according to the instructions of the Law. Samaritans believed in one God, revered the Pentateuch, and practiced a form of Israelite religion. Yet while they practiced a form of traditional Jewish religion, they also observed the religious practices of their pagan neighbors. In later centuries, animosity developed between traditional Jews and those known as Samaritans, who were hated because they were considered to be half-breeds and religiously impure observers of a perverted Mosaic religion. Samaritans were generally viewed neither as Jews or Israelites nor as Gentiles. Rather they were looked upon as a people who lived on the margins of orthodox Judaism, perhaps the lost sheep of the house of Israel, and must be avoided at all times.

The Ministry of Philip in Samaria

Philip was one of the seven chosen in Acts 6 to help oversee the care of the Grecian widows. His ministry in Samaria was the result of the scattering of the church caused by the persecution led by Saul. Luke had noted that everyone had fled Jerusalem and scattered except the apostles. Luke does not

The Ministry of Philip

indicate whether or not the apostles showed courage by staying in Jerusalem. It is possible that they stayed behind because they were not the targets of the persecution. Stephen had been executed in a mob action partly due to his perceived—if not actual—anti-temple sentiments. After all, if the Twelve did not hold anti-temple beliefs, they would likely have continued to observe the traditional times of prayer in the temple and observed the practice of Jewish piety. Perhaps those disciples who were being persecuted were believed to share the radical beliefs of Stephen. Since Stephen had been a Hellenistic Jew, perhaps the Sanhedrin believed that Hellenistic Jews posed the real and most dangerous threat and thus sought to wipe them out. Philip, also a Hellenistic Jew, fled Jerusalem and traveled to Samaria. He was the first disciple of Jesus to evangelize in this area to these people. Acts' description of Philip's ministry is reminiscent of the ministry of Jesus, especially with the use of the miracles of casting out evil spirits and healing. The text indicates that Philip's ministry brought about the conversion of many Samaritans.

During Philip's ministry there appeared a man called Simon. Simon the Sorcerer (literally, Magus), a prominent person in the Samaritan community, also believed and was baptized. He was popularly regarded as a person with divine power—a magician (literally, *magi*)—and had attracted many followers. Yet, when the crowds started to listen to Philip's preaching and observe the miracles he was able to do, many came to faith in Jesus and were baptized. Luke also says that Simon believed and was baptized. Normally when Luke uses the word "believed," he means genuine faith. Did Simon really believe or only pretend to believe?

Word got back to the apostles in Jerusalem that the Samaritans had come to faith in Jesus and had been baptized, so they sent Peter and John to evaluate the situation. Apparently the leaders of the Jerusalem church believed it was their responsibility to exercise authority over Christian activity not directly connected or controlled by the Jerusalem church. Some examples of this may be:

1. Barnabas' endorsement of the converted Saul to the Jerusalem church (9:26–30)

2. Peter's defense of the baptism of Cornelius before the Jerusalem church leaders (11:1–18)

3. Jerusalem church leaders sending off Barnabas to evaluate the Antioch church (11:19–23)

4. The decision of the Jerusalem church concerning the obligation of Gentile believers to the Law of Moses (15:1–29)

When Peter and John arrived, they learned that the Samaritans had not yet received the Holy Spirit but had only been baptized in the name of Jesus, so they proceeded to lay their hands on the people so that they might receive the Holy Spirit. Simon was particularly impressed with the apostles' power to bestow the Holy Spirit on people by the laying on of hands. Wanting the same power for himself, Simon offered the apostles money to have the power to impart the Holy Spirit to others. He undoubtedly believed that if he possessed this apostolic power his stature among the people would be significantly enhanced.

Peter responded to Simon's offer with a harsh rebuke: "May your money perish with you" (8:20, NIV). The Philips version renders Peters words: "To hell with you and you money!" Peter further accused Simon of being "full of bitterness and captive to sin" (8:23, NIV) or "in the gall of bitterness and the chains of wickedness" (NRSV). This latter comment by the apostle says that Simon's sinful attitude had seriously endangered his soul. Then Peter called on Simon to repent and ask God for forgiveness, and Simon responded by requesting prayers for his spiritual welfare.

It is tempting to conclude that Simon's conversion was insincere, done only in order to gain acceptance by the people. His true nature was seen when he tried to buy the gift of God. Nevertheless, 8:13 asserts that Simon believed and was baptized. Luke/Acts never uses the word "believe" to mean false faith. Yet it can mean inadequate faith. So, Simon may have believed the gospel message and even in Jesus as some kind of powerful divine being who brings salvation, but it is clear his faith was not adequate to understand the true meaning of discipleship. Simon was like Ananias and Sapphira, whose understanding of Christianity did not include complete surrender to the will of God. When worldly values mix with following Jesus, the result is something sub-Christian and ungodly. Later church tradition credited Simon with being the founder of a heretical Christian movement known as Gnosticism, but there is no hard evidence for this claim. The legacy of Simon can be seen in the practice known as "simony," which means the purchasing of church ministry or office.

Special Topic: The Apostles, Baptism, and the Gift of the Holy Spirit

In Acts 8:12–17, the apostles Peter and John travel to Samaria and lay their hands on the believers because they had not yet received the Holy Spirit; they had only been baptized "in the name of the Lord Jesus." This scenario seems to contradict the pattern laid out in Acts 2:38, where Peter commanded the people to be baptized in the name of Jesus Christ for the forgiveness of their sins and to receive the gift of the Holy Spirit. Based upon the Pentecost example, it seems that the Holy Spirit was promised to the baptized believer shortly after baptism or at the time of baptism. Furthermore, Acts 2 does not mention anything about the apostles laying hands on anyone. In the story of the conversion of Saul/Paul, the preacher Ananias says that he had come so Paul might regain his sight and that he might receive the Holy Spirit. Then the text mentions that his sight was restored through a miracle of healing. After Saul regained his sight, he was baptized into Christ (9:17–19). It appears here that reception of the Spirit coincided with the receiving of baptism, since Ananias told Saul that he came so that he might regain his sight and also receive the Holy Spirit. Also, the story of the conversion of Cornelius presents the scenario where Cornelius and his family received the Holy Spirit and then afterwards were baptized (10:44–47). Finally, in Acts 19:1–7 Paul baptizes twelve disciples who had previously known only the baptism of John the Baptist, and then he immediately lays his hands on them in order for them to receive the Holy Spirit. In this story, the baptized believers receive the Holy Spirit after Paul laid his hands on them immediately after their baptism.

If one is looking for a consistent pattern regarding baptism and the Holy Spirit, it appears he/she will look in vain. How does one make sense of these apparent inconsistencies, especially as it pertains to the story of the Samaritans? There are two options that are usually suggested. First, one may contend that Acts 2:38 presents the controlling pattern or paradigm for Christian conversion. Those who take this position usually assert that there is an indwelling of the Holy Spirit given to all believers at the time of their conversion or baptism, and they would claim that charismatic gifts require that the apostles lay their hands on a person in order for him/her to receive the gift. Underlying this point is that after the apostles died there were no other people who had the ability to lay hands on someone to impart the Spirit, so the charismatic gifts faded out of practice over time. Yet, nowhere in Acts is there any mention of the indwelling of the Holy Spirit. In fact, when Peter promised the gift of the Holy Spirit after baptism, what was observable to the people would have been the so-called charismatic gifts. Secondly, Ananias, who was not an apostle, laid his hands on Paul, so the imparting of that gift was not limited to the Twelve.

The second suggestion is that Acts does not contain a rigid pattern or paradigm for the imparting of the Spirit. Rather, it narrates selected cases that had a unique and important purpose in the early history of the church. In the case of the Samaritans, it is likely that Peter and John came and laid their hands on the Samaritans as a way to demonstrate their acceptance into the larger community of the church. Thus, Jewish Christians from Jerusalem, the center of traditional Jewish culture and religion, went to Samaria, to the people Jews generally considered to be unclean, ungodly, and unworthy of acceptance, and laid their hands on them so that they might receive the Spirit. In the case of Cornelius, the Holy Spirit fell on him and his family to persuade Peter and the others that God had accepted these Gentiles and that they should be baptized and be received into the church. As for the twelve disciples of John whom Paul baptized, when he laid his hands on them they received the Holy Spirit. When they received the Holy Spirit, they began to speak in tongues, thereby dramatically demonstrating God's (and Paul's) acceptance of these new believers.

The first suggestion assumes that Acts 2:38–39 is the foundation text and every passage pertaining to the reception of the Holy Spirit should be interpreted in light of it. The second approach, which this author favors, considers it important to read each narrative in Acts in light of its literary context and determine its function in the flow of Acts' overall story.

Philip and the Eunuch (8:26–40)

Following his successful ministry in Samaria, Philip was called by an angel to go south from Samaria to the desert road between Jerusalem and the city of Gaza, a once-prominent Philistine city. It was on this road that Philip encountered a man described as an Ethiopian eunuch. At this time, Ethiopia was located in the southern Nile region, more commonly known as Nubia. Acts indicates that this Ethiopian was "a court official of the Candace, queen of the Ethiopians, in charge of her entire treasury" (8:27). This person of dignity and wealth was either a proselyte (a convert to Judaism) or a God-fearer (a Gentile believer who had not fully converted). Yet Acts

The Ministry of Philip

also describes the Ethiopian as a eunuch. It was commonly believed that a castrated person was forbidden to enter the temple area and participate in worship (Lev 21:16–24; Deut 23:1). When the Ethiopian had been in Jerusalem to worship, it is very likely that he would have been restricted to the outer court of the Gentiles among the unclean, deformed, and other outcasts. The fact that the Spirit instructed Philip to go to the Ethiopian suggests that the boundaries of God's people were expanding even wider. Moreover, this story may have been an example of the fulfillment of the promise of Isaiah 56:3–5 that in the messianic age all outcasts would be included in God's kingdom.

> Do not let the foreigner joined to the LORD say,
> "The LORD will surely separate me from his people";
> and do not let the eunuch say,
> "I am just a dry tree."
> [4] For thus says the LORD:
> To the eunuchs who keep my sabbaths,
> who choose the things that please me
> and hold fast my covenant,
> [5] I will give, in my house and within my walls,
> a monument and a name
> better than sons and daughters;
> I will give them an everlasting name
> that shall not be cut off.

Isaiah continues with a similar promise to the foreigners who bind themselves to the Lord (56:6–7a), then he concludes the oracles with these words:

> for my house shall be called a house of prayer
> for all peoples.
> [8] Thus says the Lord GOD,
> who gathers the outcasts of Israel,
> I will gather others to them
> besides those already gathered. (56:7b–8)

Somehow the Ethiopian obtained a copy of Isaiah and had been reading it. Luke states that Philip ran up to the chariot and asked the Ethiopian if he understood what he had been reading, and the eunuch replied that he needed someone to explain or interpret it for him. The eunuch had been reading from Isaiah 53, which is the last of a series of the so-called Servant Songs (Isa 42:1–4; 49:1–6; 50:4–11; 52:12—53:12). Each of these songs appears to refer to an unnamed individual. The final servant song is about someone who was to suffer and die for the sins of his people. The passage quoted in Acts comes from Isaiah 53:7–8, which focuses on the unjust death of this innocent servant of the Lord. When the Ethiopian asked for the identity of this suffering servant, Philip told him the good news of Jesus. This means that Philip identified Jesus as the suffering servant of Isaiah 53. Moreover, this also means that Jesus is the redeemer of Israel, the Messiah, the source of forgiveness and reconciliation with God. The text does not indicate whether or not the eunuch had ever heard of Jesus before his meeting with Philip. Nevertheless, this traveler came to faith in Jesus as Messiah and requested to be baptized. After his baptism, the eunuch happily returned back home to Ethiopia, convinced that he had found acceptance from God through Messiah Jesus. Philip was taken by the Spirit and reappeared some twenty miles north of Gaza on the Mediterranean coast, where he continued to evangelize until he came and made his home in the provincial capital of Caesarea.

Observations Concerning the Early Ministry of Philip

Even though Acts 9 contains the only significant narrative of Philip's ministry, the place of Philip in Acts is very important since he was one of the initiators of social and racial transition in the church. Whether or not Philip first ministered to the Samaritans, his success, along with the support of Peter and John, began the fulfillment of the commission of Jesus to be his witnesses "in all Judea and Samaria." The fact that there had been centuries of animosity between Jews and Samaritans demonstrates all the more powerfully the ability of the gospel to bring together people of different backgrounds under the banner of Christ. Additionally, since the name Samaria would likely bring to mind in many Jews the fractured state of the people of God (since the division of Israel into two nations), the Samaritan mission would serve as a powerful symbol of the beginning of the healing and restoration of Israel into one people. However, that united and restored Israel would be different from what most people expected. Thus, the story of the Ethiopian serves as a hint that the boundaries of restored Israel would be far more inclusive than anyone could have imagined. A castrated Gentile worshipper of God (possibly proselyte) was welcomed into the people of God. Moreover, the prominent activity of the Holy Spirit and an angel of

The Ministry of Philip

the Lord appearing in both Samaria and on the Gaza road further show that these transitions were the result of the work and blessing of God.

For Further Study

Important Names and Terms

- Samaritans
- Magus
- Simony
- Candace
- Ethiopia
- Servant Songs

Questions

1. How might Luke's story of the scattering of Christians be a story of the hand of God in the church?
2. Samaritans and the eunuch were the marginalized and outcast people whom Philip evangelized. Who are the marginalized people for the contemporary American church?
3. What can be learned about the work of the Holy Spirit in the church in the stories of the conversion of the Samaritans and the eunuch?

ACTS 9

The Conversion of Saul of Tarsus

Introduction

Following the two stories about Philip's trail blazing evangelistic work among the Samaritans and the conversion of the Ethiopian eunuch, Luke shifts his focus to the major antagonist of this early Jesus movement, Saul of Tarsus. The story of the conversion of Saul results not only in the removal of the leading threat against these early disciples but also in the calling of the future missionary to the larger Roman world.

Though Saul had led a vigorous campaign against the followers of Jesus, he had not been able to crush the movement. Instead, the early Christians fled Jerusalem to various places. Apparently one place where the early Christians sought refuge was Damascus, an important Aramean city located about 150 miles northeast of Jerusalem. At that time, there was a large Jewish population residing in the city, making it an attractive place for these religious fugitives. In 2 Corinthians 11:32 Paul noted that the Arabian king Aretas was in power in Damascus the year he escaped over the walls of the city in a basket. Most likely, Aretas took control of Damascus around A.D. 37. Saul's initial journey to Damascus probably took place three years earlier and before Aretas took control of the city.

Because many Jesus people had escaped capture by fleeing to Damascus, the text states that Saul received permission from the high priest to bring Christians back from Damascus. Saul sought to bring back all those who belonged to "the Way." This is the first time in Acts where Christianity is called "the Way" (see 9:2; 19:9, 23; 22:4; 24:14, 22). The author also includes the expressions "the way of God" (18:25) and "the way of salvation" (16:17). The origin of the "the Way" as a term for the Christian movement is unclear. The most likely connection can be made with the Dead Sea Scrolls, where the phrase appears multiple times as a religious expression (1QS 9:17; 10:25; 11:13).

Saul's encounter with the risen Jesus is narrated three times in Acts. The first narration (9:1–19) is Luke's version of the event. The other two versions (22:4–16 and 26:9–18) are found in the speeches he gave as part of his defense to charges against him. The text states that a light from heaven flashed around him and that he heard a voice speaking to him. Light is often associated with an encounter with God or a heavenly being (12:7), and the reader learns that the voice Saul heard was none other than the voice of Jesus. However, Luke gives no indication of any visible form of Jesus. Thus, this post-ascension appearance of Jesus from heaven is not like the resurrection appearances in the Gospels. Saul's experience here is more like a vision or a theophany. Yet, this event becomes foundational for Paul's testimony and preaching.

The risen Jesus asked, "Saul, Saul, why do you persecute me?" (9:4). Since Saul had been on his way to arrest believers in Jesus, Jesus' question indicates that the Savior identifies with his people. What they experience, he also experiences. Perhaps Jesus' identification with his people was one of the sources of Paul's doctrine of the church as the body of Christ. Rabbi Gamaliel had previously warned the Sanhedrin that their opposition to the Jesus movement could result in them becoming enemies of God if it turned out that God had been blessing and guiding it. Strangely, Saul found himself at odds with the God he had devoted his life to serving. His question, "Who are you, Lord?" (9:5) shows that he did not immediately recognize this spiritual presence as Jesus. He may have thought it was a spirit or angel. One should not read too much in Saul's use of the term "Lord"; it was simply an expression of respect, like "Sir." Most translations render 9:7 to mean Saul's companions heard a voice but did not understand it. Paul's version in 22:9 says essentially the same thing. The Greek word for "voice" (*phonei*) can also refer generally to a sound or noise. So, it is not certain whether the reader is to conclude that these men heard Jesus' voice but couldn't understand what was being said, or that they simply heard some indistinct sound.

The story then states that the risen Jesus commanded Saul to go to the city to learn of God's will for him. The visionary experience had left Saul temporarily blind, so he would need to be guided to the place Jesus appointed. As he waited in Damascus, this sightless former persecutor of Christians spent his time in prayer and fasting. Jesus had sent Saul to Damascus to be instructed by a disciple whose name was Ananias. It is important to note that Luke wants his readers to know that it was the Lord (Jesus) who arranged for Saul's conversion. Saul had a vision of the risen Jesus, who commanded him to go to Damascus, and Ananias also had a vision of Jesus commanding him to go to the house of Judas, where Saul was staying. Moreover, both Saul and Ananias had separate visions concerning the other. The point is that Jesus orchestrated events that led to Saul's conversion.

The text indicates that Ananias expressed concerned to the Lord because of Saul's reputation as a persecutor of believers. Yet, the Lord assured him that Saul was "chosen to bring my name before Gentiles" (9:15). So, the Saul story is more than a conversion story: it is a calling of Saul to witness to the Gentile world. The language here and in the parallel accounts has the characteristics of a prophetic calling. Paul himself described his conversion as a prophetic call (Gal 1:13–16). It is not necessary to decide whether he was converted or called—the two go together. For example, the call of Isaiah (Isaiah 6) brings together the themes of confession, repentance, and forgiveness of sins with a call to mission. Ananias went to Saul and told him he was sent so that Saul might regain his sight and be filled with the Holy Spirit, which in Acts is the power to witness (1:8).

The Ministry of Saul in Damascus (9:20–25)

After Saul had regained his sight and was baptized, he began to proclaim in the synagogues of Damascus that Jesus was the Son of God. No doubt, part of Saul's proclamation included an interpretation of the Old Testament, which concluded that the Messiah was in fact Jesus. Due to Saul's effectiveness in preaching, the opposition within the Jewish quarter grew to a point that his life was in danger. However, Saul escaped the city in a basket through an opening in the wall. Paul mentioned his escape from Damascus in the basket in 2 Corinthians 11:32–33 and stated that King Aretas of Damascus had been trying to kill him. Perhaps the hostility of Aretas had been caused by Jewish antagonists who accused Paul of being a troublemaker (Acts 24:2–8).

In addition to 2 Corinthians 11:32–33, Paul referred to the above events in Galatians 1:13–20, in which he mentioned a three-year stay in Arabia and a return to Damascus prior to going to Jerusalem to be introduced to the church. Based on these passages, the following chronology of events may be suggested:

The Conversion of Saul of Tarsus

1. Saul encountered the risen Jesus on the Damascus road and was eventually converted.
2. Saul engaged in a brief preaching ministry in Damascus immediately following his conversion.
3. Saul went to Arabia, where he stayed for three years.
4. Saul returned to Damascus, resumed his ministry, and escaped the city in the basket.
5. Saul traveled to Jerusalem to be introduced to the church.

Saul Introduced to the Jerusalem Church (9:26–31)

When Saul arrived in Jerusalem, the disciples were understandably afraid and suspicious of him. Perhaps some thought that this so-called conversion was simply a ploy to get access to the followers of Jesus whereby he could then arrest and imprison them. True to the meaning of his nickname, Barnabas ("Son of Encouragement") openly supported and endorsed Saul as a genuine follower of Jesus. Acts states that Barnabas told the story of Saul's encounter with Jesus on the Damascus road. His words convinced the Jerusalem disciples to accept Saul as a brother in the Lord. Once accepted by the Jerusalem church, Saul began to preach about Jesus in Jerusalem. Saul's preaching produced hostility with some of the Hellenists or Grecian Jews. Ironically, these may have been the same people who opposed Stephen (6:8–9). So in a way, Saul, who had participated in the death of Stephen, took the place of the church's first martyr. Consequently, his life was in danger. Thus, in order to save his life, the Jerusalem church sent Saul away to Tarsus, a city in the Roman province of Cilicia. Paul states in Galatians 2:1–10 that fourteen years after his flight to Cilicia, he went up again to Jerusalem. Scholars are is disagreement as to what Paul exactly meant by "after fourteen years," and also which visit to Jerusalem Paul was referring to. In this author's view, Paul is referring to the years between his conversion (c. 35) and the Jerusalem conference following the first missionary journey (c. 49). Nevertheless, whatever he meant, it is clear that Paul had been away from Jerusalem for some time, living and working in Cilicia and, later, Syria. Acts does not indicate how long Saul was in Tarsus or what he did while he was there. It is reasonable to assume that he preached in the synagogues that Jesus was the Messiah. Acts concludes this segment of the narrative by noting that, due to the conversion of Saul, persecution of believers had ceased and the church throughout Judea, Galilee, and Samaria experienced peace and numerical growth.

Summary of Peter's Ministry Outside of Jerusalem (Acts 9:32–43)

Luke then turns from the story of the conversion of Saul to the expanding ministry of Peter. When the great scattering of believers took place following the death of Stephen, many fled to distant regions to escape persecution. In Acts 8, Peter and John travel to Samaria to welcome Samaritan believers into the Jesus community. At some point after that, Peter traveled about twenty-five miles west of Jerusalem to the town of Lydda. While there, he met and healed a man named Aeneas who had been paralyzed for eight years. The description of the healing is reminiscent of the healing miracles of Jesus, except the words of healing were "Jesus Christ heals you" (9:34). These words indicate that the true healer is Jesus, who continues to minister through his people.

The story of the raising of Tabitha is the first example of a resurrection miracle in Acts. The story takes in Joppa, about ten miles northwest of Lydda. As with the story of the healing of Aeneas, the raising of Tabitha recalls the earthly ministry of Jesus. The Gospel of Luke contains only two resurrection miracles of Jesus. One is the raising of the son of the widow of Nain (Luke 7:11–17); the other is the raising of the daughter of Jairus (Luke 8:40–56). The two stories in the Gospel involve children or young adults, but in Acts Peter apparently raises an adult woman. In fact, this adult woman is described by Luke as one whose life was filled with "good works and acts of charity," especially to the poor and widows. The raising of Tabitha has more in common with the story of the daughter of Jairus. One interesting connection is in the words of Jesus. To the deceased Tabitha, Peter said, "Tabitha get up" (Acts 9:40), and to the daughter, Jesus said, "Child get up" (Luke 8:54). In Mark's version of the raising of the daughter, Jesus said in Aramaic, "Talitha cum," and Peter's words to Tabitha would have been in Aramaic, "Tabitha cum" (Mark 5:21–43). Perhaps Luke wanted the reader to understand that even the resurrection miracles of the apostles were empowered by the living Lord of the church, Jesus of Nazareth.

Afterwards, Peter went to the home of Simon the Tanner and stayed with him. The fact that Peter chose to stay with one whose profession required the handling of animal carcasses—which made one ceremonially unclean according to Jewish law and tradition (Num 19; Lev 11:24–40; 17:15)—may indicate that Peter was slowly changing his understanding of the role of law and tradition with its global implications for the gospel.

For Further Study

Important Names and Terms

- Damascus
- Aretas
- Lydda
- Tabitha
- Decapolis
- Aeneas

Questions

1. Saul's conversion is recorded three times in Acts. Why would the author repeatedly narrate this event? Is there a theme Luke was emphasizing through these texts?
2. Write an outline of a chronology of Saul's life, beginning with his conversion and ending with his first missionary journey.
3. Peter appears to be the first of the twelve apostles to leave Jerusalem to exercise his ministry. How do the later stories of Peter reveal his personal and spiritual growth?

ACTS 10:1—11:18

The Conversion of Cornelius

The Vision of Cornelius (10:1–8)

THE STORY OF THE conversion of Cornelius is the second important narrative in Acts. Like the conversion of Saul, the story of the conversion of Cornelius is told or referred to three times, with the first and longest account in Acts 10 and shorter versions in 11:1–18 and 15:7–11. Also like the conversion of Saul, the conversion of Cornelius was as much about what God did as it is about the actions of the individuals. In the story, Cornelius was visited by an angel who commanded him to summon Peter to his house, and Peter also had a vision of a great white sheet, which prepared him to go into a Gentile's home and share the gospel with him. Further, as Peter was speaking, the Holy Spirit fell upon Cornelius and his household, which Peter interpreted as a sign that God had accepted them and that they should be baptized. Thus, God brought together people who would normally not have had anything to do with each other.

Caesarea is described as the home of Cornelius the centurion. Located some thirty miles north of Joppa, Caesarea Maritima was the Roman capital of Palestine and, as such, it contained the residence of the Roman procurator/governor. Cornelius is described as a centurion of the Italian cohort. A cohort was a battalion of about six hundred soldiers, within which a centurion commanded about one hundred. The Italian cohort apparently was a collection of volunteer Italian-born Roman citizens who had been stationed in Syria by Rome. One should not miss that Cornelius was a Roman—likely an Italian Roman—who also was a commander of native Roman soldiers. Nothing more symbolized the arm of Roman oppression and the object of Jewish hatred than the Roman army. This Roman army officer was the one to whom Peter would preach the gospel.

Cornelius is also described as devout and God-fearing; this likely means he was a Gentile who accepted the Jewish faith short of full conversion. So, Cornelius had embraced the faith in the one God of Israel and the moral teachings of Torah, but he did not submit to circumcision or observe traditional dietary and purity Jewish regulations. Luke points out two aspects of Cornelius' piety: (1) he gave (alms) generously to those in need, and (2) he prayed regularly, i.e., at the appointed times of prayer according to the Jewish daily calendar. In fact, it was at the Jewish time of prayer that an angel appeared to him. The text indicates that the angel appeared to him around 3 p.m. (or during the ninth hour)—one of the hours of prayer. The angel told him that his prayers and acts of generosity had become a memorial to God. The Greek word for "memorial offering" was used in the Septuagint to refer to the Jewish vegetable offering. The angel said that Cornelius's prayers and good works "ascended as a memorial before God," no doubt alluding to the ascending of the sweet aroma of a sacrifice accepted by God. One should not miss this important statement; an unclean Gentile was recognized by God as if he were Jewish or a spiritual proselyte. The second part of the angel's message is the command to find "Simon who is called Peter" (10:5) and bring him back in order to listen to his message. In obedience to the angel, Cornelius sent men to find Peter and bring him back.

The Vision of Peter (10:9-16)

On the next day Peter had his divine encounter. According to Acts, Peter's experience took place at noon (literally, the sixth hour), which was not the usual time of prayer. The text states that Peter went on the roof to pray at this unusual hour, and while praying he became hungry, which set the stage for his upcoming experience. Then Peter fell into a trance. The Greek word for "trance" is *ekstasis* and is used in the Septuagint to refer to the ecstatic experiences of the early prophets. It was a common word in Greek literature used to refer to certain kinds of religious experience. The word appears three times in Acts, twice regarding Peter's experience in Joppa (10:10 and 11:5) and once as a descriptive of Paul's encounter with the risen Jesus (22:17). The point is that Luke intended for the reader to conclude that Peter's trance-like experience was an encounter with the living Lord. Here Peter, in a visionary state, saw something like a great white sheet descending from heaven. On this sheet Peter saw all kinds of animals, specifically those regarded as unclean in the Torah. Peter then heard a voice from heaven ordering him to kill and eat. While in his trance, Peter resisted the command from heaven by pointing to his loyalty to the Law. Perhaps Peter believed the Lord was testing his loyalty to the Law, or perhaps the voice he heard was really not the voice of God but of the Evil One. However, the voice insisted that God had made all foods clean. Was such a thought completely new to Peter? Possibly not. While Luke says nothing definitively, according to Mark, Jesus introduced the idea that all foods were clean (Mark 7:14–23). Acts portrays Peter as struggling between loyalty to his past versus loyalty to the present word of God. This vision happened three times, which indicates the importance of this for Peter.

The Sending of Peter to the house of Cornelius (10:17–23)

Even though Peter knew he had experienced something supernatural—a voice from heaven instructing him to eat unclean food that was no longer unclean—he did not know the ultimate significance of his experience. Was the message of the vision only that God had nullified the food laws of the Torah, or was there some additional meaning? The reader knows that Peter's experience meant more than simply a change in food laws. It had to do with Peter's attitude toward Gentiles.

The men who were sent by Cornelius arrived in Joppa looking for Peter. After searching, they came to the home of Simon the Tanner, where Peter had been staying. Luke indicates that when they arrived the Spirit directed Peter to go with these men sent from Cornelius. As with the story of the conversion of Saul, so here Luke shows that the bringing together of a Roman soldier with a Jewish preacher of Jesus was the work of God. Luke indicates that the Spirit had directed Peter to go with the messengers and also had sent these men to bring Peter back with them. When Peter met the messengers at the door and heard their message, he invited them into the house. The very fact that Peter invited these Gentile messengers into the house where he was staying was evidence of Peter's growth in understanding the universal implications of the gospel.

The Meeting of Peter and Cornelius (10:23b–33)

The next day, Peter traveled with the messengers to the home of Cornelius in Caesarea. When Cornelius with family and friends gathered to meet and greet Peter, they fell down before Peter, but he stopped them and said, "I am only a mortal" (10:26). These first words by Peter indicate his newly enlightened heart. Like most Jews, Peter had believed it was against Jewish law to associate with Gentiles. However, his vision of the unclean animals taught him how one was to treat his fellow human beings and that no one should be regarded as unclean simply because of race. Cornelius then proceeded to rehearse for him his encounter with the angel, including his sending of the men to Joppa. Now that Peter was present, Cornelius indicated that the entire household was ready to hear a word of God from him.

Peter's Sermon (10:34–43)

In response, Peter declared that he now understood that "God shows no partiality" (10:34). The Greek word for "show partiality" is *prosopoleimpteis*, which literally means "a face receiver." To receive a face means to pay regard to one's looks or external circumstances rather than the inner qualities of the heart. Consequently, race, nationality, gender, color of skin, social station, and a host of other variables are of no ultimate consequence to God. Instead of these superficial qualities, what God desires are people who "fear him and do what is right." Luke notes that Cornelius was a man who feared God (10:2) and did righteous acts through his alms and prayers. God wanted Cornelius to hear the gospel because his faith and piety had prepared him to come to faith in Jesus as Lord and Messiah.

The text proceeds with a sermon by Peter. Like the other speeches in Acts, what is presented here is a summary and/or reduced version of a much longer message. One of the interesting characteristics of this sermon is that it is a summary of the life of Jesus that is consistent with the chronology of events found in the Gospels, especially the Synoptic Gospels. The following is an outline of Peter's sermon:

1. The ministry of John the Baptist
2. The anointing of Jesus with the Holy Spirit and power (his baptism)
3. References to healings and exorcisms probably during his Galilean ministry

4. Jesus' ministry in Judea and Jerusalem
5. The crucifixion of Jesus
6. The resurrection of Jesus
7. Jesus' commission of the apostles to preach
8. Invitation to repentance and faith

A few comments on Peter's message are appropriate here. In 10:36, Peter said to Cornelius, "You know the message he sent to the people of Israel." Peter assumed that Cornelius was at least aware of Jesus and his disciples. Peter also assumed that Cornelius was aware of some elements of Jesus' ministry whether in Judea or Galilee. Though Peter did not explicitly mention Jesus' baptism, he stressed the anointing of the Holy Spirit—a clear allusion to Luke's description of Jesus in Luke 4:18 by means of Isaiah 61:1. Additionally, Luke's account of Peter's sermon describes Jesus' ministry as "doing good and healing all who were oppressed by the devil" (10:38). This is consistent with the Third Gospel's portrayal of Jesus as a compassionate Messiah who had power over evil spirits.

Peter stressed the role of the apostles as witnesses to Jesus, who ministered to those in need, who was killed by being hung on a tree, and who was raised to life by the power of God. The NIV translates 10:39b as, "They killed him by hanging him on a cross." While the crucifixion of Jesus on the cross is certainly what the writer is referring to, the Greek word *xylos* usually means "tree." The use of this word is most likely a strong allusion to Deuteronomy 21:23. An English translation of the Septuagint version of the relevant portion of Deuteronomy 21:23 reads, "for every one that is hanged on a tree is cursed of God." The same Greek word for tree is found both in Acts 10:39 and Deuteronomy 21:23. Peter's sermon, therefore, associated Jesus' death by crucifixion with the Deuteronomy passage concerning hanging on a tree because of the importance of the divine curse. Jesus was killed as one who was under a curse by God.

Next, Peter said Jesus was raised on the third day and was seen only by those who were chosen to be witnesses of him. The reference to "the third day" shows how firmly embedded this detail of Jesus' resurrection was in the tradition of the early church. Also, that the risen Jesus only appeared to believers who would serve as witnesses perhaps indicates that the resurrection was not primarily intended to be proof of Jesus' identity, but rather the sign of the culmination of God's work in him and the transition of Jesus to a place of exaltedness by God's side—a sign only understandable by faith. Peter stated that Jesus appeared to those who ate and drank with him, which stressed the reality of Jesus' bodily resurrection. It was the risen Jesus who commissioned the apostles to preach and testify of him and offer forgiveness of sins to all who believe in him.

The Conversion of Cornelius—The Gentile Pentecost (10:44–48)

As important as the sermon of Peter was, the significance of this story for Luke was not, however, the content and structure of Peter's sermon but the resulting conversion of Cornelius and his household. That is why the author immediately moves from a summary of the sermon to a description of the Holy Spirit falling upon the household of Cornelius. The author states that Peter's speech was interrupted by the noise of the outpouring of the Spirit. According to 10:44, the Spirit "fell upon all who heard the word." The presence of the Spirit was manifested in the "speaking in tongues and extolling God." In other words, the Spirit came upon these Gentiles in the same way it did to believers on the day of Pentecost. In 11:17, Peter said the apostles at Pentecost received the Holy Spirit *when they believed*. It is likely, therefore, that Cornelius and his family came to faith in Jesus at the preaching of Peter, and thus received the Spirit.

In response to this, Peter concluded that these Gentiles had received the Spirit just as the disciples at Pentecost had. God accepted the faith and love of these Gentiles as he had Peter and his fellow Jewish believers in Jesus. Consequently, Peter felt he had no choice but to baptize in water these who had received God's Spirit. This is the only instance of the administration of baptism after one had received the gift of the Holy Spirit. There have been two suggested explanations for this apparent anomaly. First, some suggest that this was a sign to Peter and brethren that God had accepted the Gentiles. Certainly Peter's words indicate this: "Can anyone withhold the water for baptizing these people who have received the Holy Spirit just as we have?" (10:47). Second, it has also been suggested that this event was also a sign to Cornelius and family that God had accepted them. While the text does not explicitly explain it in that way, this is a reasonable interpretation.

The conversion of Cornelius has sometimes been called the Pentecost of the Gentiles; since what happened to the Jewish believers in Jerusalem in Acts 2 happened here to believing Gentiles. The implication of this event is that the borders of the church had been redrawn and widened to include all people who believe in Jesus.

Peter's Defense of His Evangelization of Cornelius and Family (11:1–18)

News of the conversion of Cornelius and his family spread very quickly throughout this primitive Jewish church. The implications of the inclusion of Gentiles into the Christian community were profound and reached critical mass in Acts 15 at the well-known Jerusalem conference. At this point, the primary criticism came from those Luke labeled "the circumcised believers." Their concern was that Peter entered the house of a Gentile and ate with them. Many observant Jewish believers refused to enter a Gentile's house or eat his food out of concern for becoming ritually unclean. Peter's defense focused on the activity of God as he retold the story of his vision of the large sheet with the unclean animals, the voice from heaven warning him not to call unclean what God had cleansed, the meeting of the servants of Cornelius, the preaching to this Gentile family, and the Holy Spirit coming upon them. It is interesting to note that the name "Cornelius" is not mentioned once in Peter's defense in 11:1–18, nor is there any reference to the piety and good works of Cornelius. Peter's defense for going to and eating with the Gentiles did not rest on human faith or piety but on the decisive action of God. The initiative of God gave Peter no option; he had to accept this Roman soldier. Peter's argument was apparently effective, for the response of his hearers was to worship God, declaring that

> "God has given even to the Gentiles the repentance that leads to life." (10:18)

While Peter defended his going to and associating with a Gentile, it is ironic that Paul notes in Galatians 2:11–13 that Peter (or Cephas) withdrew from the Gentile brethren out of fear or respect for the scruples of more conservative brethren from James in Jerusalem. Explanations for this apparent inconsistency on the part of Peter have been varied. Perhaps this at least shows that social change in the church, as in society as well, never happens on a straight ascending line. This story in Acts is important because it shows that significant progress had been made in the formation of a global fellowship of believers in Jesus. Nevertheless, Acts shows that there was still work to be done: the establishment of a racially integrated community of faith.

For Further Study

Important Names and Terms

- Cornelius
- Centurion
- Cohort
- Septuagint
- Caesarea

Questions

1. How significant is it that the first Gentile conversion in Acts was through the work of Peter and not Philip or Paul?
2. What importance does the story of Cornelius have for understanding the rest of Acts?
3. Summarize all the places where divine intervention played a role in the Cornelius story.

ACTS 11:19—12:25

The Antioch Church/The Persecution of Herod Agrippa

The Church in Antioch (Acts 11:19-26)

THE ESTABLISHMENT OF THE Antioch church marks a major transition point in the narrative. In 11:19, Luke refers back to the scattering of disciples during the persecution following Stephen's death. Prior to this, Luke narrated the following events (8:5—11:18):

1. Conversion of the Samaritans
2. Conversion of the Ethiopian Eunuch
3. Conversion of Saul
4. Healing of Aeneas and raising of Dorcas by Peter
5. Conversion of Cornelius
6. Establishment of the Antioch church

It may be that Luke intended for the reader to understand these events to have happened essentially concurrently rather than sequentially. In any case, it is clear that the establishment of the Antioch church is meant to be the result of the persecution and scattering of believers in Jesus. Note the events leading to Antioch summarized by the author:

1. Many Christians were scattered and fled to Antioch at the time of persecution.
2. Most of them spoke only to Jews.

3. Some Christians from Cyprus and Cyrene spoke to Greeks in Antioch.
4. A great number of people came to faith, undoubtedly both Jew and Gentile.

Antioch of Syria was the third largest city in the empire with a population of approximately 800,000. Like most large Graeco-Roman cities, Antioch was known to be a place of lax morals. This city included a large and influential Jewish community as well as many Gentile proselytes. In other words, Antioch was a city where there was significant interaction between Jews and Gentiles, making it a likely location for the first integrated church.

Evangelism in Antioch

The message of these early evangelists was a proclamation of "the Lord Jesus," with no mention of Jesus as Messiah. The word "Lord" (*kyrios*) was an important title in Greek culture given to a god. In a culture that would not have understood the Jewish concept of Messiah, these early evangelists apparently sought to connect with their Gentile hearers by using language that made sense to them, the language of the culture around them. The result of the message was, "The hand of the Lord was with them" (10:21). This means the Lord approved of their evangelistic efforts, and their work resulted in many conversions.

Barnabas Sent to Antioch

Up to this point in the narrative, the word "church" appears to refer exclusively to the faith community in Jerusalem. Since this new faith was born in Jerusalem, it seems that the leadership of the Jerusalem church assumed oversight for this messianic movement. That is why Peter and John were sent to Samaria in Acts 8:14–17 to lay their hands on the newly baptized believers. In essence, the Samaritan Christian community was under the leadership of the Jerusalem church. Moreover, until the work in Antioch began, all evangelistic work seems to have been carried out under the auspices of Jerusalem. It is clear that the Antioch evangelism work had been carried out apart from the guidance and endorsement of the Jerusalem church. Therefore, when the leadership in Jerusalem heard about the community of believers in Antioch, they sent Barnabas to examine and evaluate the work. Barnabas was an appropriate and fortunate choice. He was a native of

Cyprus, which means he was a Hellenistic Jewish Christian, one who would better understand a Jew's life outside of Palestine. Furthermore, the author already indicated that Barnabas, as his nickname suggested, had a reputation as an encourager. The text indicates that Barnabas faithfully fulfilled his role as an encourager and spiritual leader:

> When he came and saw the grace of God, he rejoiced, and he exhorted them all to remain faithful to the Lord with steadfast devotion; [24] for he was a good man, full of the Holy Spirit and of faith. And a great many people were brought to the Lord. (11:23–24)

Barnabas encouraged this young church and stayed on as a minister. He also went to Tarsus to find Saul and bring him back to work with him. While it is possible to interpret 11:25 to refer to a one-year ministry, Paul in Galatians 1:18–2:1 suggests that he and Barnabas were in Antioch for longer than one year.

Disciples Were First Called "Christians" in Antioch

In Acts 11:26, the author states that the believers in Antioch were called "Christian" for the first time. The word "Christian" appears only three times in the NT (Acts 11:26; 26:28; 1 Pet 4:16). In Acts 26:28, King Herod Agrippa asks if Paul thought he could make him a Christian after his brief defense speech, and 1 Peter 4:16 speaks of suffering as a Christian. So, in two of the three passages, the name "Christian" is either spoken by an unbeliever or is part of the motivation of unbelievers to persecute followers of Jesus. Literally, "Christian" refers to one who is a follower of Christ. Throughout Christian history, there have been at least three theories for the origin of the name "Christian."

1. The name "Christian" was a divinely given name.
2. The designation of the name "Christian" was in fulfillment of prophecy (i.e., God's people will be given a new name).
3. The name "Christian" was used to identify and/or distinguish believers from both pagans and Jews.

A brief evaluation of each theory is appropriate: (1) It has been suggested that the act of being given a name implies that it was done by the apostles or prophets at the direction of God. Such an interpretation can only be inferred and not clearly demonstrated.

(2) The theory regarding prophecy fulfillment is based largely on an interpretation of Isaiah 62:1–5:

> For Zion's sake I will not keep silent, and for Jerusalem's sake I will not rest, until her vindication shines out like the dawn, and her salvation like a burning torch. ² *The nations shall see your vindication, and all the kings your glory; and you shall be called by a new name that the mouth of the LORD will give.* ³ You shall be a crown of beauty in the hand of the LORD, and a royal diadem in the hand of your God. ⁴ You shall no more be termed Forsaken, and your land shall no more be termed Desolate; but you shall be called My Delight Is in Her, and your land Married; for the LORD delights in you, and your land shall be married. ⁵ For as a young man marries a young woman, so shall your builder marry you, and as the bridegroom rejoices over the bride, so shall your God rejoice over you.

There are several problems with this theory. First, there is no quote or reference to this Isaiah text anywhere in Acts, unlike in other places where Luke clearly identifies a fulfillment of prophecy. Thus, if Luke does not declare this a prophecy fulfillment, why should we make that conclusion? Second, Isaiah's oracle in chapter 62 presents several names for the people of God, but nothing approaching "Christian" can be found. It is best to regard this theory, however attractive to Christians, to the category of "eisegesis," a reading into the text of one's preconceived opinions.

(3) The last theory suggests that the name "Christian" was given by unbelievers as a way to identify this new community of faith. Moreover, since there were similarities between the church and the synagogue or between those who believed in Jesus and Jews who did not believe in Jesus, the name "Christian" would serve as a helpful distinguishing label. It may be that some unbelievers called believers in Jesus "Christians" as a form of insult, but likely it was more often a form of identification.

Yet, it is interesting that Luke introduces the name "Christian" at this point in the narrative. It may be that, historically, the name originated in the city of Antioch at this time, which means that Luke is simply giving us historical information. Perhaps also, Luke wants his readers to see that the title "Christian" was given to the first Jesus community that embodied God's global vision for the gospel. The Antioch church was the first multicultural, multiracial church, and only such a church could justly be labeled "Christian."

The Antioch Church Responds to News of a Famine (11:27–30)

At this point in the narrative, there are two churches: the Jerusalem church and the Antioch church. The Jerusalem church was a thoroughly messianic Jewish community, while the Antioch church included believers in Jesus from both the Jewish and Gentile communities. The cultural differences between these two churches could not be greater. In that context, Luke tells us that "prophets came down from Jerusalem to Antioch." The presence of prophets was a sign of the presence of the Spirit in the church. And the prophets' presence in Antioch suggests God had accepted this new type of church. Agabus, one of the prophets, announced the coming of a famine throughout the world. Luke added that this worldwide famine took place during the reign of the Roman emperor Claudius (41–54). Josephus mentions that a particularly rough famine came upon Judea around 44–46 (*Antiquities of the Jews*, 20. 51–53). Perhaps this is the famine crisis that the Antioch church responded to.

While Acts does not indicate if Agabus exhorted the Antioch church to send relief to their brethren in Jerusalem, the church seems to have immediately responded to the need. Luke describes the Antioch collection in this way: "The disciples determined that according to their ability, each would send relief to the believers living in Judea; this they did, sending it to the elders by Barnabas and Saul" (11:29–30).

The text states that each disciple made his/her own decision as to how to individually respond to the crisis. Therefore, each one gave according to his ability; no set amount was required to be given. In other words, the Antioch church demonstrated the practice of freewill offerings of individual members who had joined together for a common cause. Moreover, this act of compassion by the Antioch church should also be seen as an expression of fellowship with the Jerusalem church. While these two churches were very different in member composition and perspective, they shared a common faith in Jesus and regarded each other as part of God's global redeemed community.

After the collection was made, the Antioch church sent Barnabas and Saul to deliver their gifts to the Jerusalem elders (11:30). This is the first time the word "elders" is mentioned in Acts in connection with the church. More will be said about this word in the discussion of chapter 15. One brief observation here: In Acts 4:32–34; 5:1–2; and 6:1–4, money collected to help the poor was "laid at the apostles' feet." Here in 11:30, Barnabas and Saul brought the collection to the elders. Perhaps in the early days of the church as described in Acts 2–5, the apostles functioned more like the elders of a group. Then in Acts 6, the apostles stated that they could no longer devote time to managing the distribution of relief for the poor and called for the appointment of seven men, who were both honest and spiritual, to oversee the collection and distribution. While these seven have often been called the first deacons, it may be that they were precursors to the first elders.

The Persecution of Herod Agrippa (Acts 12)

The Martyrdom of James and Imprisonment of Peter (Acts 12:1–5)

The story of Acts then shifts to the second major persecution of the church. The scene opens with a summary of the execution of the apostle James at the orders of King Herod. James is the first and only apostle whose death is described in Acts, and his death was because he "belonged to the church" (12:1). The King Herod in Acts 12 is called Herod Agrippa by Josephus. He was the grandson of Herod the Great and son of Aristobulus, who died when Herod Agrippa was four years old. Agrippa's mother sent him to Rome to be brought up and educated. During his time there, he became close friends with the imperial family. Consequently, his friend Emperor Claudius made him a king in 41 (essentially ruling over the territory of his grandfather, Herod the Great), and he remained in power until his death in 44. Agrippa was apparently a popular king with the Jews because of his support for the beliefs of the Pharisees.

According to Acts, Herod had James killed with the sword, which probably means that he was beheaded. The execution of James pleased the Jewish leaders and thus marked the end of the fragile peace in Jerusalem between the church and the Jewish leadership. Perhaps this new persecution was a reaction of the church's new policy toward Gentiles. Then Herod arrested Peter with plans to also execute him. Apparently, Herod's policy was to control or eradicate this Jesus movement by eliminating the leaders. The author makes a point to inform the reader that Herod planned to try Peter after Passover. As Jesus was arrested, imprisoned, tried, convicted, and executed during the Passover season, so Herod intended to do the same to the leading apostle Peter. Yet, in contrast to the destructive plans of King Herod, the church, writes Luke, prayed fervently to God for Peter.

The Deliverance of Peter (12:6–17)

While awaiting his fate, Peter is portrayed as helpless in contrast to the power of King Herod. With a soldier on each side of him, bound with two chains, and additional soldiers guarding the entrance to Peter's cell, there appeared no possible way for the apostle to escape. Like Jesus on the boat during a dangerous storm, Peter is pictured sleeping, perhaps confident of God's protection. Then, the text states that an angel appeared and awakened Peter by forcefully tapping or striking him on the side and instructing him to get up, put on his clothes and sandals, and follow him out of the prison. Immediately the chains on Peter fell off, and Peter got up and followed the angel out of the prison while the guards were all mysteriously asleep. When Peter, who at first thought he was in a trance or having a vision, realized that he had actually escaped prison undetected, he went to one of the primary meeting places of the disciples, the house of Mary the mother of John, who was also known as Mark. Earlier Luke noted that the church had been praying fervently for Peter when he had been imprisoned. That group was still praying when the apostle arrived at the door of the house.

A servant girl named Rhoda answered the door and, to her surprise, saw Peter standing before her. When she told the disciples who had been praying for Peter, they thought she was delusional. Strangely, they said she may have seen Peter's angel. Perhaps this means they thought God, through an angel, had sent a message to the church from the apostle or that the vision of the angel was an indication of Peter's death. When the church went to see who was at the door and saw Peter, the text indicates they were amazed; they had not expected to see him. Peter then quietly told them how he had miraculously escaped from the prison and that they should tell James (the brother of Jesus) and the other fellow believers what had happened. After that Peter departed to an unnamed place.

I have three observations about the story of Peter's release from prison. First, this portion of the story showed the church faithful in prayer but apparently not expecting Peter's release. Had they been praying for his release but didn't really believe it would happen, or had they been praying that Peter would remain courageous and faithful to the gospel in face of the threat of death? The latter is more likely. Second, the departure of Peter to another place signals the end of Peter's leadership of the Jerusalem church and the beginning of James, the Lord's brother, as the new leader. Third, this story shows that despite the threats of a powerful king, God was still in control and would allow nothing and no one to thwart or defeat his plan for the world. Church tradition states that eventually Peter was arrested, convicted, and executed by the Roman government. But while God's purpose for James the apostle had been fulfilled in his death, God still had work for Peter to do. The second half of this story will show the demise of the king who had tried to destroy the church.

The Death of Herod (12:20–33)

The second half of the story concerning Herod Agrippa has little to do directly with Peter and the church. The importance of the story is that Herod accepted praise from others as if he were a god and suffered the consequence for his arrogance. The story opens with Herod angry with the people of Tyre and Sidon of Phoenicia. The reason for his anger is unclear; perhaps there were territorial disputes or complaints about food distribution. At a critical point in the story, Herod appears in public on the day of his meeting with Tyre and Sidon clothed in royal robes and seated on a platform. From his platform Herod delivered a speech, and the people declared his speech to be the "the voice of God." In Josephus' description of this event, he wrote that the crowd's ascription of divinity to Herod was due to the glorious appearance of his clothing. Nevertheless, Acts states that the angel of the Lord struck him dead because he did not give praise to God. According to Josephus, Herod Agrippa likely died of worms after suffering great pain for a period of five days (*Antiquities of the Jews*, 19. 343–51).

Following the death of Herod Agrippa, Luke observed: "But the word of God continued to advance and gain adherents" (12:24). Though Herod had sought to eliminate the Jesus movement, the end result was that Herod's reign and life were forfeited and the church continued to move forward reaching more and more people. This shows the triumph of the gospel despite threats and challenges to the work of the church. Luke implies that the crisis with Herod Agrippa took place while Barnabas and Saul were in Jerusalem delivering the gifts from the Antioch church. If that is correct, then following Herod's death, they returned to Antioch, taking with them John, who was also known as Mark. This prepares the reader for the next major division of the narrative: the carrying of the gospel to the entire

Roman world through the missionary efforts of Barnabas and especially Saul, who would later be called Paul.

For Further Study

Important Names and Terms

- Christian
- Claudius
- Herod Agrippa
- Rhoda
- Tyre

Questions

1. The name Christian appears only three times in the New Testament (Acts 11:26; 26:28; 1 Pet 4:15). Obviously, this term was not the earliest or the favorite of the early church. According to the New Testament, what terms or names were more frequently used than Christian? What do these other terms signify?

2. How important is prayer in Acts, especially in those places that describe the disciples gathered for prayer? Read 1:12–16; 4:24–31; 6:1–7; 8:14–17; 12:1–17; 13:1–3.

3. What theme or themes are highlighted in the story of Herod in chapter 12? How do any of these connect to the larger story of Acts?

ACTS 13:1—21:17

The Missionary Journeys of Paul

ACTS 13–14

Paul's First Missionary Journey

The Call of Paul and Barnabas (13:1–3)

CHAPTERS 13–20 FOCUS PRIMARILY on the missionary journeys of the apostle Paul. The first journey is narrated in chapters 13–14. As a kind of break from the travel narratives, Acts 15 summarizes the issue debated and events that occurred during the Jerusalem conference. Paul's second journey is described in 16:1—18:22, and the third journey essentially is found in 18:23—21:16. It is within these chapters that the narrative summarizes the spread of the gospel throughout the Mediterranean world. This globalization of the gospel began in Antioch of Syria, where Barnabas and Saul received their call to travel to distant lands with the message of Jesus.

Luke described the leadership of the Antioch church as consisting of prophets and teachers; there is no mention of elders. In addition to Barnabas and Saul, the text mentions three people who served as leaders in Antioch. (1) Simeon called Niger: "Niger" was likely a Latin nickname that referred to his dark complexion and may suggest he came from Africa. (2) Lucius of Cyrene: The city of Cyrene was an old Greek colony located in North Africa. (3) Manaen: Acts states he was a member of the court of Herod the tetrarch. This Herod is thought to have been Herod Antipas, who was a son of Herod the Great. It may be that this Manaen was the grandson of another Manaen who was a supporter of Herod the Great.

While these men were gathered for worship, perhaps with the entire church, Luke says that the Holy Spirit called Barnabas and Saul for a special work. The Spirit's call probably came through one of the prophets, and it happened while they were engaged in worship and fasting; perhaps the group was seeking the will of God. After they were certain that the Holy

Spirit had truly spoken and called Barnabas and Saul to this mission, the group laid their hands on Barnabas and Saul as a sign of empowerment of the Holy Spirit and of their commission by the church. Then the church sent Barnabas and Saul off to distant places to proclaim the message of Jesus.

After Barnabas and Saul had been commissioned by the Antioch church, they traveled to the port city of Seleucia (sixteen miles southwest of Antioch) and set sail. This first journey had three major parts to it: (1) the ministry in Cyprus; (2) the ministry in Roman Asia (also known as Asia Minor); (3) the ministry in Roman Galatia.

The Ministry in Cyprus

The island of Cyprus was approximately 60 miles from Seleucia. The island is about 140 miles long and 60 miles wide. Acts mentions only two cities by name that Barnabas and Saul visited on Cyprus: Salamis and Paphos. Salamis was the commercial center of the island and the eastern seat of the provincial government. The narrator mentions that these two missionaries proclaimed the word in the synagogues there. This likely suggests the evangelistic strategy of Barnabas and Saul: they focused on preaching in the synagogues to win their Jewish brethren to faith. Nothing is specifically said at this point about evangelizing non-Jews, though it is possible the missionaries also shared the gospel with Gentiles. The text also notes that Barnabas and Saul were assisted by John, likely the one also known as Mark. Acts states that this mission team traveled westward across the island to Paphos, where the real drama of their mission in Cyprus took place. Paphos was located on the west side of Cyprus. It was the primary location of the governmental headquarters. In Paphos, Barnabas and Saul encountered two men. Luke describes the first as a Jewish magician, or sorcerer, and false prophet named Bar-Jesus. The Greek word for "magician" is the same used to describe Simon the magician/sorcerer in Acts 8:9–13. Bar-Jesus apparently served as an adviser to Sergius Paulus, the proconsul (the provincial governor) of Cyprus. The text describes Sergius Paulus as an intelligent man who wanted to hear the message of Barnabas and Saul. One minor theme of Acts is that the gospel is credible to reasonably intelligent and fair-minded persons. Bar-Jesus, or Elymas (the sorcerer's other name), sought to prevent Sergius Paulus from listening to Barnabas and Saul. He may have thought that he would lose credibility and influence if the proconsul accepted the gospel. At this point the writer says that Saul, who was by that time also known as Paul, rebuked Elymas and told him he would be temporarily blinded. It is ironic that Paul, the former persecutor of the church who was temporarily blinded when he encountered the risen Jesus, told Elymas that the Lord would strike him blind for a period of time as punishment for his opposition to the gospel. Also, the parallels between this story and that of Peter with Simon the Sorcerer are interesting. For example, both Peter and Paul delivered a very strong rebuke to the sorcerer. Here Paul called Elymas a child of the devil. When Sergius Paulus saw that Elymas went blind just as Paul predicted, the text says "he believed" (13:12), which in Acts is usually an expression for becoming a follower of Christ. This conclusion is supported by the text's inclusion of his amazement at the teaching about Jesus. With this event, the first Roman official comes to faith in Jesus.

From this point forward in Acts, the narrator uses the name Paul to refer to this missionary companion of Barnabas. It should be noted that the name Paul should not be understood as Saul's new Christian name. Rather, Paul chose to take on the Hellenistic version of his Hebrew name since he was ministering in Gentile territories.

Ministry in Asia Minor (13:13–52)

From Cyprus, the missionary team sailed some one hundred miles north from Paphos to the port city of Perga, a Roman colony and leading city in the province of Pamphylia. The author notes it was from Perga that John Mark left the missionary company and returned home. No explanation is given for John's apparently sudden departure. Perhaps John, who was a relative of Barnabas (Col 4:10), was unhappy that Paul had taken over the leadership of the mission effort from Barnabas. It has also been suggested that Paul's willingness to preach to Sergius Paulus and accept him as a fellow believer in Jesus without requiring circumcision may have been too much for this young Jewish Christian. One thing is clear: John's departure was viewed by Paul as evidence of his unreliability for mission work, an issue which would cause a major rift between Paul and Barnabas. Another note of interest is that in 13:13 the text reads, "Paul and his companions." This is the first time Paul's name is placed first when the missionary team is mentioned.

From Perga, the missionary team traveled to Antioch of the province of Pisidia. Antioch of Pisidia was located approximately 3,600 feet above sea level. The route Paul and Barnabas likely traveled would have been a very steep and difficult hike. On the Sabbath, Paul and Barnabas went to the local synagogue for worship and were invited to speak. It was not uncommon for a traveling Jewish teacher to be asked to say a few words of encouragement in the synagogue. What follows is the first major sermon or speech by Paul in Acts. This speech has some similarities with Peter's sermon in Acts 2 and his remarks in Acts 3. I have divided the sermon into two major parts: (a) God has been active in guiding and providing for his people from the beginning to the coming of Jesus (from Moses to Jesus); (b) the death and resurrection of Jesus is the culmination of God's saving work and the demonstration that Jesus is God's Son and our Savior.

(a) *God has been active in guiding and providing for his people from the beginning to the coming of Jesus* (13:16–25). The consistent feature of this section is the exclusive emphasis on the activity of God in the history of salvation. Note the italicized portions of the text:

> The God of this people Israel *chose our ancestors* and *made the people great* during their stay in the land of Egypt, and with uplifted arm he *led them out of it*. [18] For about forty years *he put up with them in the wilderness*. [19] After *he had destroyed seven nations* in the land of Canaan, *he gave them their land* as an inheritance [20] for about four hundred fifty years. After that *he gave them judges* until the time of the prophet Samuel. [21] Then *they asked for a king; and God gave them Saul son of Kish*, a man of the tribe of Benjamin, who reigned for forty years. [22] When *he had removed him, he made David their king*. In his testimony about him he said, "I have found David, son of Jesse, to be a man after my heart, who will carry out all my wishes." [23] Of this man's posterity *God has brought to Israel a Savior, Jesus*, as he promised.

Virtually all the verbs in this section show God as the primary actor in Israel's story. Another theme that emerges from this section is the continuity of the gospel with the faith of Israel. The God who chose the patriarchs to be the ancestors of Israel, delivered Israel from slavery, and led them through the wilderness to the promised land where Israel would be built into a nation is the same God who brought Jesus to the world. Moreover, even Jesus was descended from the royal line of David and came into the world as Savior in fulfillment of the promise of God to Israel. The implication at this point is that faith in Jesus is not a negation of one's Jewishness but the fulfillment of the hopes of Israel.

(b) *The death and resurrection of Jesus is the culmination of God's saving work and the demonstration that Jesus is God's son and our savior* (13:26–41). This second part of Paul's sermon intends to show that Jesus is the goal of history, since it was through him that God accomplished salvation for humankind.

Paul called his message a "message of salvation." Jesus' death is described by Paul as both a great tragedy of human injustice and a fulfillment of God's plan of salvation. Those who had opposed Jesus did not really know who he was, yet they condemned him to death. Paul singled out the Jews—most likely the Jewish leaders—as the most culpable for this injustice since, he said, "they asked Pilate to have him killed" (13:28). Though the death of Jesus was horrible and wrong, it was in some mysterious way part of God's plan of salvation. Moreover, God reversed their evil intentions by raising Jesus from the dead, who appeared to his companions over many days. Consequently, these companions, known otherwise as the apostles (note Paul did not include himself here as an apostle), are the witnesses of Jesus. In verse 23 Paul calls Jesus "Savior." The strong implication is that the resurrection of Jesus confirmed that Jesus is, in fact, Savior and Messiah.

To further support his argument that the death and resurrection of Jesus fulfilled God's plan of salvation, Paul cited from Psalm 2, Isaiah 55, and Psalm 16. First he quoted from Psalm 2:7 in order to argue that Jesus is truly the Son of God. Interestingly, Paul referred to this psalm as the "second psalm"—clear evidence that by his time the book of Psalms had already been arranged and edited in something like its current form. The loose quotation from Isaiah 55:3 was given to further connect Jesus to the Davidic dynasty and the covenantal promises associated with it. The third quotation, from Psalm 16:10, was cited early in Peter's Pentecost sermon (2:27) and is an affirmation of God's faithfulness to his promises concerning the Messiah, who is Jesus. Paul (13:36–37), like Peter (2:29–31), emphasized the distinction between the mortal King David from his risen and divine descendant, Jesus. Paul concluded his sermon by announcing that forgiveness of sins is available through faith in Jesus. For his Jewish audience, Paul singled out forgiveness even for sins that could not be forgiven under the Law of Moses; these would be deliberate sins. The Greek word for "set free" or "freed" can also be rendered "justified" or "acquitted." Then Paul gave a solemn warning to his hearers not to ignore his message of salvation. He quoted from Habakkuk 1:5, which is a warning to Israel that God is about to send the Babylonians to punish Israel and inflict great suffering on them because they had been unfaithful to the Law. Paul's use of this quote could simply be a warning against unbelief or it could be a veiled reference to the destruction of Jerusalem.

In response, the people wanted to hear more (13:42–52). So, when Paul and Barnabas arrived the next Sabbath, they discovered a large crowd (Luke says "almost the whole city"; 13:44), including Gentiles along with Jews gathered to hear more about Jesus. But Luke states that the Jews in the crowd "were filled with jealousy (13:45) and sought to undermine and discredit the message of Paul and Barnabas. Acts' use of the word "jealousy" suggests that the Jews were upset that the Gentiles had been attracted to the preaching of Paul and Barnabas and that these missionaries clearly had accepted them. It may also be that since the Gentiles outnumbered their Jewish neighbors, the leaders of the local synagogue did not like being overwhelmed and outnumbered by Gentiles. This led the synagogue leaders to influence the crowd against Paul and Barnabas and force them to leave. Paul indicated that the Jewish opposition had forced him to go to the Gentiles, and with that Acts presents to the reader the missionary strategy of Paul, which was to first go to a synagogue in order to win some Jewish believers to Jesus. To stress this, Luke quotes from Isaiah 49:6, one of the so-called Servant Songs of Isaiah. In Isaiah 49, the Lord's servant is clearly Israel who, among other things, was called to be a light to the nations. That mission, according to Acts, is to be fulfilled in the mission efforts of Paul and Barnabas.

Eventually, the opposition from within the synagogue proved too much for Paul, so he left the synagogue and went to evangelize non-Jewish people. We have already discussed some of the reasons why Jews might not have been supportive of Paul, but it is less clear how these Jewish opponents were able to persuade both Gentile women and men of high social standing and power to persecute them and drive them out of the city. Perhaps the opposing Gentiles had come to believe that Paul and Barnabas were political troublemakers—a charge that would appear other places and times during Paul's missionary career. As previously mentioned, in 13:13 Paul is listed for the first time before his traveling companions. Similarly, in 13:42 the phrase "Paul and Barnabas" appears for the first time. Clearly, the focus of the text has shifted to Paul as the lead person, and that may represent a change in his stature during this missionary journey.

Ministry in Galatia (Acts 14)

The story of Paul and Barnabas' ministry in Antioch of Pisidia closes with the missionaries shaking the dust off their feet, giving the people of Antioch one last warning against unbelief, and leaving the city. Their next destination was the city of Iconium, some ninety miles east of Antioch. Iconium was located in the traditional region of Lycaonia, which was in the southern portion of the Roman province of Galatia. Most likely, Paul's canonical letter to the Galatians was written to churches of southern Galatia. Though Paul and Barnabas told their Jewish opponents in Antioch of Pisidia that they were going to the Gentiles (13:46) in Iconium, these missionaries seemed to go directly to the local synagogues and engaged in teaching there first. Initially, it seemed that the response to the preaching of the gospel was very positive from both Jews and Gentiles (likely from the God-fearers), but eventually opposition arose against Paul and Barnabas. Apparently, the leaders of the synagogue began to openly oppose the preachers, successfully turning both many fellow Jews and God-fearer Gentiles against them. Consequently, Paul and Barnabas were forced to evangelize outside the synagogue, likely on the street and in people's homes. The author doesn't specifically indicate how long they were in Iconium; he simply states that "they remained for a long time, speaking boldly for the Lord" (14:3).

The work and message of Paul and Barnabas caused considerable controversy in the city. The opposition against them grew so intense that a plot against their lives by means of stoning was discovered, forcing them to leave the city.

In 14:4, the author mentions a controversy concerning "the apostles." The word "apostle" is only used three times in Acts to specifically refer to Paul and Barnabas (14:4, 6, 14). A survey of Acts reveals that Paul is never called an apostle apart from his work with Barnabas or other missionary associates. Acts never considers Paul or any other person a replacement apostle for the martyred apostle James, nor is Paul regarded in Acts as something like the thirteenth apostle. While Paul in some of his letters strongly defends his apostolic calling and authority, in Acts the word "apostles" when used of Paul and Barnabas suggests their roles as missionaries, as people who had been sent out on a mission. In the case of Paul and Barnabas, they were called and sent out by the Holy Spirit as communicated and endorsed by the Antioch of Syria church.

Paul and Barnabas left Iconium and went to Lystra, which was eighteen miles from Iconium. The absence of any reference to a synagogue in Lystra and the fact that Paul's only recorded speech contains no quotations or allusions to the Old Testament nor even to Jesus has led many scholars to conclude that there was likely no synagogue and possibly no Jews living in the city. If there was a synagogue in Lystra, Luke makes no mention of

Living Lord, Empowering Spirit, Testifying People

it. What is emphasized is the reaction by the people of Lystra to a healing miracle by Paul. The text indicates that Paul came upon a man who had been lame from birth. When Paul realized the man had faith, he commanded the man to stand up, and the lame man sprang or jumped up and starting walking. This story has similarities to Peter's healing of a lame man at the gate of the temple in Jerusalem (3:1–10). In both stories, the man had been lame from birth, both Peter and Paul commanded the lame man to stand up, and both texts make mention of the faith of the lame man. After Peter healed the lame man, the onlooking crowd was so excited that the divine power to heal did not come from Peter's own goodness or power but from faith in Jesus (3:10–13). Similarly, the healing of the lame man in Lystra caused people to believe that Paul and Barnabas were gods who had come down to them. They called Barnabas "Zeus" and Paul "Hermes." The people's belief that Zeus and Hermes had come down to earth seemed to have been based on local beliefs and stories that these gods had visited their area. In an attempt to honor these visiting gods, the people of Lystra brought bulls and garland to offer sacrifices to Paul and Barnabas. Yet Paul and Barnabas dramatically stopped the proceedings by tearing their clothes as a sign of dismay and anguish and declaring to them they were not gods but humans like them (again, similar to Peter's response in 3:12–13).

What follows is Luke's brief summary of Paul and Barnabas' message concerning the one true God. While the message is described as gospel or "good news" (14:7), the sole focus of the message here is on God the creator and sustainer of the universe. There are four things said about the true God: (1) the living God is the creator of all things; (2) God has allowed all nations to go their own way, i.e., without direct revelation or divine law; (3) God has revealed his goodness in creation by showing kindness by providing the world with rain which produces abundant crops (thus, if God's goodness is revealed in creation, creation itself may be also regarded as good); (4) with these crops God blessed humanity with food and joy. From these remarks, it may be concluded that since God has revealed himself in a good and fruitful creation, humankind should have recognized the hand of this good creator. God is not completely unknowable. Furthermore, if creation is good and fruitful and if God has provided humanity with food and joy, then it is clear that the true God is a good and kind God who cares about his creation.

This is the first example in Acts of a sermon or speech given specifically to a pagan audience. Paul's longer speech in Athens is another example of early evangelization of Gentiles (17:22–31). The strategy seems to be to introduce people to the one true God before introducing Jesus as the Son of God. While it seems that the apostles were able to convince some of the people of Lystra, at least enough to stop sacrifices to Paul and Barnabas, their success was short lived. Luke states that Jews from Iconium and Antioch came to Lystra and turned many against the apostles. That Jews from Iconium and Antioch traveled to Lystra to persecute Paul shows the intense level of hostility towards Paul and Barnabas that existed among these opponents. Moreover, these opponents not only came to Lystra and poisoned the people against the apostles, they also stoned Paul and dragged him outside the city and left him for dead. Fortunately Paul's wounds were not fatal, and he recovered enough to return to the city.

On the next day Paul and Barnabas left Lystra and traveled about eighteen miles to the town of Derbe. Acts says little about what happened in Derbe, other than that Paul and Barnabas were more successful there in winning converts to Jesus. At some point, the apostles returned to the cities Lystra, Iconium, and Antioch, where, despite the opposition to Paul and Barnabas, there existed a group of believers in Jesus. During these second visits, Paul and Barnabas sought to strengthen and encourage the disciples in their faith and to appoint elders in each church. Drawing from their own experience, it was important to remind and encourage these new disciples that following Jesus requires a faith and commitment that can endure any challenge and/or persecution one may face. Secondly, in order to assist these new churches to remain faithful, the apostles appointed elders in each church to provide leadership, guidance, and wisdom to face the days ahead. Paul and Barnabas no doubt believed that religious communities do much better when there are people in place to lead, guide, teach, and, when necessary, correct.

Paul and Barnabas completed the final portion of their trip by passing on through Antioch of Pisidia to Perga and then to Attalia, from where they found a ship and sailed on to Seleucia, and then returned to their home church in Antioch of Syria. While they were in Antioch, Paul and Barnabas reported to the Antioch church the results of their mission trip. The wording here is instructive: "When they arrived, they called the church together and related all that God had done with them, and how he had opened a door of faith for the Gentiles" (14:27). Note that the apostles stated that it was God who actually accomplished those works with (or through) them and that it was God who had opened a door of faith for the Gentiles. In other words, the work of Paul and Barnabas among the Gentiles was really the work of God in and through them. God is the primary actor who was accomplishing his plan of bringing the message to the world. Not only, as the old hymn declares, is the gospel for all, but the God of Abraham is for all people. The question is: can believers from different cultures, races, nationalities, and even traditions embrace and put into practice this divine vision and plan? For Luke, this question is addressed in the next chapter, concerning the Jerusalem conference.

For Further Study

Important Names and Terms

- Cyrene
- Manaen
- Paphos
- Seleucia
- Elymas
- Sergius Paulus
- Lystra
- Hermes

Questions

1. Drawing from Paul's sermons in Acts 13–14, what were the characteristics of Paul's missionary or evangelization methods?
2. How is God's nature and work described in Acts 13–14?
3. How do Acts 13–14 present guidelines for church ministry in different cultures?

ACTS 15:1–35
The Jerusalem Conference

The success of the missionary journey of Paul and Barnabas had become for some in the church a source of controversy. The controversy had to do with their ministry to the Gentiles. Actually, this was a controversy that had been growing for some time, beginning with the conversion of the Roman centurion Cornelius. Cornelius' conversion initially caused a stir but was eventually accepted after Peter pointed to the outpouring of the Holy Spirit upon this Roman and his family as a sign of God's approval. However, it appears that by this time the number of Gentiles in the church had grown significantly. Moreover, it had become apparent that eventually Gentiles would outnumber Jews in the church. If this demographic change occurred as some likely feared, the implications for the church would be far-reaching and profoundly unsettling for some Jewish disciples. Jews who had become believers in Jesus usually brought with them both a strong religious and moral foundation. The Torah had provided for Jews both a theological foundation of faith in the one creator God and moral principles based on the Ten Commandments and other laws. Consequently, most Jewish converts did not have to change their belief in the one true God or repent of some moral sin, but simply accept Jesus as the Messiah. For them, Jesus brought to fulfillment their faith and religious identity. In contrast, many Gentiles who had been converted did not bring similar religious or moral foundations. In fact, Gentiles were generally and justifiably regarded by Jews as people who led immoral lives.

For this and other reasons, many Jewish Christians concluded that it was necessary for Gentile converts to observe the Mosaic Law as a condition for membership in the church. Specifically, this meant that a Gentile male who believes in Jesus must also submit to circumcision; that both men and women converts must eat only ritually pure/clean food; that they avoid contact with any unclean thing, animal, or person; and that they observe the Sabbath and other Jewish holy days. The argument for this position goes something like this:

1. If Jesus is the Jewish Messiah, then to be Jesus' disciple one must take on the Jewish faith and tradition that Jesus observed.
2. Jewish Christians who observe the Law are not permitted to associate with Gentiles believers if, through neglect of the Law, they are unclean.
3. The moral integrity of the church will suffer unless Gentiles are required to keep the Law.
4. The requirements for admission into the church should be the same for converting to Judaism, with the addition of faith in Jesus and baptism. Thus, one must essentially become a Jew in order to become a Christian

The Jerusalem Controversy

Acts states that some Judean brethren came to Antioch insisting that Gentile converts be circumcised in order to be saved. As a result, a fierce debate arose between Paul and Barnabas and representatives from what Luke labels "the sect of the Pharisees" (15:5). In order to settle this dispute, the leadership of the Jerusalem church called for a general conference to discuss the matter.

Special Topic: Comparison between Acts and Galatians

Acts' description and chronological placement of the Jerusalem conference has been a subject of debate among New Testament scholars for over a century. The issue of dispute has to do with whether Galatians 2:1–10 describes the Jerusalem conference. The majority of scholars believe it does. However, the chronology of Galatians does not seem to agree with Acts. The issue hinges on the number and nature of Paul's post-conversion visits to Jerusalem. Acts describes four visits to Jerusalem by Paul:

1. The introduction visit of Paul the new convert (9:26–30)
2. The so-called famine visit of Paul and Barnabas (11:27–30)
3. The Jerusalem conference (15:1–35)

The Jerusalem Conference

4. The visit following Paul's third missionary journey (21:17–40)

In contrast, Galatians mentions the following visits to Jerusalem:

1. The introduction visit of Paul the new convert (1:13–20)
2. Paul and Barnabas' visit to Jerusalem to describe their ministry and preaching to the Gentiles (2:1–10)

Note that Paul in Galatians makes no clear mention of the famine visit (Acts 11:27–30). Either Paul omitted a reference to the famine visit or perhaps the visit of Paul and Barnabas described in Galatians 2:1–10 might have actually been the famine visit of Acts 11:27–30. If, however, Galatians 1:13–20 is the famine visit of Acts 11:27–30, then the visit in Galatians 2:1–10 is very likely the Jerusalem conference visit of Acts 15. If Galatians 2 describes the famine visit, then it is probable that Galatians was written before the convening of the Jerusalem conference, making it likely the earliest of Paul's writings. The fact that Galatians is partly concerned with whether or not a believer in Jesus had to be circumcised has convinced many scholars in North America and Great Britain that Galatians was the first of Paul's letters, written sometime before the Jerusalem conference. However, other scholars are persuaded by the similar characteristics between the Jerusalem visits described in both Acts 15 and Galatians 2 suggest that Galatians 2:1–10 must be describing the Jerusalem conference. This latter interpretation assumes that Galatians was written sometime after the conference, perhaps as late as Paul's third missionary journey. While not pertinent to the study of Acts, this author has assumed that Galatians 2:1–10 is describing the Jerusalem conference of Acts 15.

The Conference

According to the author, there was considerable discussion and debate about the relationship of Gentiles Christians to the Mosaic Law. The implications of this debate were profound, since it was concerned with the nature of this Jesus movement: was it to be simply another sect of Judaism or a world religion? In theory, Judaism was a universal and inclusive faith. In fact, there are prophetic texts that envision a world unified in faith in God and observance of Torah. But in reality, Judaism had become a religion deeply tied to the Jewish people. At the heart of Jewish identity and religious conviction is the respect and observance of the Law of Moses. A group of disciples Luke calls "the sect of the Pharisees" stated that it was "necessary for them [Gentile believers] to be circumcised and ordered to keep the Law of Moses" (15:5). In response to this, the author presents summaries of responses by Peter, Paul and Barnabas, and James.

Peter's speech was in favor of inclusion of Gentiles without the Law. He argued that God had called him to preach the gospel to the Gentiles. Moreover, God demonstrated his acceptance of Gentiles by giving the Holy Spirit, just as he did on Pentecost. Peter concluded that God had forgiven them on the basis of their faith. Therefore, the apostle argued that the church should not add to Gentiles the burden of the Law that even their fellow Jewish brothers were not able to carry. The point is that God saves people by grace and not on the basis of ethnic identity or ritual performance.

The second response came from the ones who had been on the mission field, Paul and Barnabas. Luke doesn't summarize specific things that were said but simply notes that these two missionaries reported all the miracles that God did through them during this journey. Why stress the miracles? The reason seems to be that these miracles were evidence that God had blessed their mission among the Gentiles, and if God blessed them in their work, he must be pleased with the conversion of Gentiles without the obligations of the Mosaic Law.

The third and final response came from James, presumably the brother of Jesus. His main point was that the inclusion of the Gentiles was consistent with the vision of the prophets. He reinterpreted Amos 9:11–12, which refers to the restoration of Israel, as a prophecy about the inclusion of Gentiles. James concluded his remarks by recommending the following:

a. Gentiles should not be forced to take on the Mosaic Law, i.e., circumcision and dietary and purity codes.

b. Gentiles should abstain from "things polluted by idols and from fornication and from whatever has been strangled and from blood" (15:20)—probably things associated with idolatry.

James' first recommendation clearly affirmed that Christianity was a worldwide religion, not tied to any race or nationality. The second recommendation is harder to interpret. Some of the restrictions seem to be associated with Jewish dietary scruples while others may be connected to pagan religious practices. The prohibition against sexual immorality might simply be a reminder of the disciple's calling to sexual purity, or it could be referring to practices often associated with idolatry. Whatever the exact truth,

James was recommending that Gentile brethren respect Jewish ceremonial sensitivities and avoid the impurities often associated with paganism. The conference concluded with the leaders agreeing to James' recommendation. To communicate their decision, a letter was drafted that was to be read to all the churches. Judas, also known as Barsabbas (1:23), and Silas (future missionary companion of Paul) were commissioned by the Jerusalem church to read the letter to the church in Antioch, which they did and exhorted the congregation.

For Further Study

Important Names and Terms

- Sect of the Pharisees
- Barsabbas
- Silas
- Food polluted by idols
- Jewish purity codes

Questions

1. What are the primary challenges for communities that promote diversity?
2. What significance does the story of the Jerusalem conference have for the church of the twenty-first century?
3. Peter said that people are saved by the grace of the Lord Jesus. How can this truth break down walls of prejudice?

ACTS 15:36—17:15

Paul's Second Missionary Journey: Troas, Philippi, Thessalonica, and Berea

Plans for the Second Missionary Journey

AFTER THE CONCLUSION OF the conference, Paul recommended to Barnabas that they revisit those new communities of faith they established during their missionary tour. No doubt the decision of the conference to accept Gentile believers as truly fellow disciples was part of the motivation behind Paul's motivation to visit them. As this portion of the narrative unfolds, it is clear that Paul's intention for this second mission tour was more than simply visiting and encouraging existing new churches: it was also to establish new ones. Evidently, Paul's original plan was to go west across Asia to Ephesus, the wealthiest and most important city in Roman Asia. Most likely he wanted to establish some kind of base of operations in this city from which he could evangelize much of the entire province. However, those plans were altered by what Acts describes as the Holy Spirit and/or the Spirit of Jesus. Instead of Ephesus, Paul would travel northwest to the city of Troas, then sail across the Aegean Sea to evangelize in both the provinces of Macedonia and Achaia.

Before the journey could begin, though, a sharp disagreement arose between Paul and Barnabas over the young man known as John and Mark. Barnabas had wanted to bring Mark along on this second trip, but Paul strongly disagreed because he didn't trust him. For some reason Mark, who had accompanied them on the first trip, abruptly left the mission trip and returned home. Paul regarded Mark's actions as desertion, but Barnabas apparently wanted to give the young man another chance. Paul may have thought that Barnabas was not being objective since John Mark was his relative, perhaps a cousin or nephew (Col 4:11).

As mentioned above, Acts does not give a reason for Mark's desertion of the mission. It might be that he was unhappy that Paul had taken over as the new leader of the mission team. It has also been suggested that Mark felt uncomfortable with Paul's broad acceptance of Gentiles. Since no reason is given for Mark's action, it can be assumed that Mark's motivation was of no interest to the writer. Instead, the author of Acts is interested in that fact that a dispute occurred between Paul and Barnabas followed by a break-up of this evangelistic partnership.

There are two things to notice from this story. First, the author does not tell the reader which of the two had been in the wrong; the writer does not take sides. Second, the focus of the story shifts to Paul and his new companions Silas and Timothy. The reader learns that Barnabas took John Mark with him to Cyprus, but nothing is said about their work. In contrast, the rest of Acts is devoted to the work that Paul and others did in spreading the gospel in eastern Europe, western Asia, and eventually Rome. The point seems to be that even internal disputes between church leaders did not stop God from accomplishing his purposes and the forward movement of the gospel message.

Paul and Silas Travel on from Syria to Cilicia and Points West

The text states that Paul, Silas, and Timothy went through the provinces of Syria and Cilicia, no doubt to churches established during the first missionary journey. Then the missionary team went on to Derbe and Lystra. These cities, along with Iconium, were located in the region of Lycaonia but had been joined with the traditional territory of Galatia to form the province of Galatia.

Luke indicates that while Paul was in Lystra he added Timothy to the missionary team. This young man is described by the author as a son of a Jewish woman and a Greek man. Perhaps because the male authority in a first-century household usually determined the religion of the household, Timothy had not been circumcised, though he apparently was taught to believe in the God of Israel. However, since Timothy was to be ministering to Jews, Paul felt it was necessary to have Timothy circumcised. Most likely, the common definition of a Jew included having at least a Jewish mother. If this was the attitude of the Jews in Lystra, then Timothy was in violation of the Law of Moses. Only by having Timothy be circumcised could Paul or Timothy hope to have any credibility in the synagogue. It has been noted that Paul in Galatians 2:1–10 strongly argues that he is opposed the imposition of circumcision on Gentile believers because doing so, in effect, denies the gospel of justification apart from works of the Law. But Paul's opposition to circumcision as a requirement of the gospel is different from Paul's support of circumcising a Jew to better work and evangelize other Jews.

The Macedonian Call

It was mentioned above that Paul had originally planned to travel westward to Asia and evangelize the eastern side of the Aegean Sea. Yet, his plans were changed and not by his own doing. Acts states that the Holy Spirit (16:6) did not allow Paul to preach in Roman Asia (modern day Turkey) and stopped him from going northward to Bithynia (16:7), located near the southern edge of the Black Sea. Paul eventually was led to Troas at the far northwestern corner of the region (16:8). Then the reader learns of Paul's vision of a man from Macedonia asking for help (16:9–10). Paul and his missionary team concluded that this vision was a sign from the Lord that they should go to Macedonia to preach the good news.

Acts 16:10 states: "When he had seen the vision, we immediately tried to cross over to Macedonia, being convinced that God had called us to proclaim the good news to them." This verse contains the first of what are commonly known as the "we" passages, called so because of the presence of the first-person pronouns "we" and "us." The "we" passages first appear in the narrative about Paul's ministry in Philippi (16:10–17) and then cease after Paul leaves Philippi. They reappear during Paul's third missionary journey after he and his associates left Philippi and continue through the remainder of Acts (20:5–15; 21:1–8; 27:1—28:16). The "we" passages of Acts have been the subject of much thought and reflection. However, one thing seems clear about them: they show that the originator of these texts was an eyewitness of and participant in some of the events in Paul's career.

Ministry in Philippi

After a brief stopover at the island of Samothrace, this missionary team landed at the port city of Neapolis. Nothing is said about any evangelistic work in this city. The first significant stop for Paul and his associates was the ancient city of Philippi, which was named after King Philip of Macedon, the father of Alexander the Great. Acts states that Philippi was a Roman colony, which means the city promoted all things Roman. The city observed Roman law, patterned its city constitution after that of Rome, used Latin for all official communication, and in general demonstrated loyalty to the emperor and the empire. Philippi was the leading city of one of the four districts within the province of Macedonia. Since nothing is said in Acts of Paul visiting a synagogue, it is generally assumed that there were very few Jews in the city; a minimum of ten men were traditionally required to establish a synagogue.

Conversion of Lydia and Her Household

Up to this point in Luke's story, Paul's pattern of activity in a new mission site was to visit the local synagogue and seek an opportunity to either speak to people during the service or to arrange more informal gatherings for instruction. However, since there apparently was no synagogue in Philippi, Paul and company found a place of prayer on the Sabbath. It was here Paul met Lydia and later baptized her and her family. And with the conversion of Lydia and her household, the gospel had for the first time made a foothold in Europe. Acts does not tell us if Lydia was Jewish, though that might be inferred by her attendance at a Sabbath prayer service. Yet, she may have been a Gentile worshipper of God, what were known in some circles as "God-fearers." According to Acts, Lydia was from the city of Thyatira, a city located in Roman Asia. Lydia is further described as a businesswoman since she was a seller of purple cloth. Also, since Lydia is mentioned without reference to a husband, it is likely that she was a widow. At her request, Paul and his associates stayed in her home. It is also very possible that the Philippian church met in her home.

Exorcism of the Spirit from the Slave Girl

After establishing Paul's relationship with Lydia, Acts narrates the fascinating and brief story of the deliverance of a girl from some kind of spirit. The reader should not miss that the social status of the lowly slave girl contrasts with that of Lydia, a wealthy businesswoman. Most translations describe this spirit as a "spirit of divination," while a few others (notably the NIV) focus on the spirit's ability to predict the future. The Greek word behind this is *pythoma*, which is the source of the English word "python." This spirit may have been associated with the sacred site of Delphi, a place in Greece where a female prophet called "the pythia" uttered oracles from the god Apollo about the future. In ancient Greek mythology, Delphi had been guarded by a large dragon or snake.

When Paul arrived in Philippi, it is possible that *pythoma* had come to mean other things, usually associated with fortunetelling or ventriloquism—in general, something associated with making money. In fact, the girl in this story seems to have been exploited by her owners as a type of fortuneteller for profit. According to Acts, the slave girl was proclaiming Paul and Silas to be "slaves of the Most High God" (16:17). The title "Most High God" was an ancient pagan expression for the supreme deity within a pantheon of deities. It was adopted by Israel to refer to the supremacy of their God over the gods of the nations. Did this girl believe in the God of Israel? Or is Luke describing an evil spirit's recognition of God and Paul as God's servant through the voice of this slave girl? The latter is more the point here. This is also the best way to understand the girl's announcement of Paul's message of the way of salvation. This story has some important similarities with the story of the deliverance of the demon possessed man known as Legion in Luke's Gospel (8:26–37). In both stories, a person is possessed by a powerful spirit or host of spirits. When Jesus or Paul approached the possessed person, he or she spoke of the "Most High God." Then, after the possessed person had been delivered by the authority of Jesus' word or power, the interested observers were upset in part because the source of their livelihood had been removed—by the death of the swine in the Luke, and the healing of the slave girl in Acts. In this brief story, Luke shows the conflict between the gospel and Hellenistic religion and/or pagan prophetic oracles, and the power of Jesus over religious commercialization and demonic powers.

The Imprisonment of Paul

As a result of delivering this girl from the power of this spirit—and by extension the abusive control of her owners—Paul and Silas were arrested and thrown in jail. The text notes that Paul and Silas were attacked for being "Jews" and threats to the social order. The use of the word "Jews" shows that prejudice against Jews existed in the early years of Christianity. As the Roman Empire expanded and took on more and more peoples of different nations, cultures, and faiths, there emerged in some quarters a concern about the purity of Italian blood and culture. The Jews' commitment to the belief in one supreme God and that this God was king of all nations appeared to some as a threat to the culture and values of the empire. In a city that took great pride and effort to be loyal to Rome, any potential threat to the Roman way would have to be eliminated. Consequently, Luke records that Paul and Silas were stripped of their clothing, flogged, and thrown into prison, probably for one night. In the prison, Acts mentions that Paul and Silas were praying and singing hymns to God and that other prisoners were listening to them. Perhaps they evangelized in prison through the medium of worship. It is also possible that Paul and Silas were thanking God for being considered worthy of suffering for the name of Jesus. At any rate, their worship lasted past midnight, when a great earthquake struck the city.

The Conversion of the Jailer

The violent shaking of the earthquake caused the prison doors to break loose and open. The jailer, who assumed that the prisoners had escaped under his watch, had decided to take his life rather than face the humiliation of public disgrace. But he was prevented from committing suicide by Paul, who assured him that all the prisoners were still there. No doubt surprised and relieved, the jailer asked, "What must I do to be saved?" (16:30). What the jailer meant by his question is unclear, but he must have known that Paul was a religious teacher. Paul's response suggests he understood the jailer to be asking about spiritual salvation, for he replied, "Believe on the Lord Jesus and you will be saved, you and your household" (16:31). After talking with them about Jesus, the jailer took them to his home to care for their wounds and then was immediately baptized along with his household.

Following a night of joyful and thankful worship, Paul made it clear he wanted nothing less than a public apology for being mistreated and denied his legal rights as a Roman citizen. This is the first time that Paul's Roman citizenship is mentioned. To be a Roman citizen was a privilege that provided rights not available to non-citizens. Nothing is said of his citizenship in his letters, though perhaps he implies it in Philippians 3:20, where he writes of a believer's heavenly citizenship. Paul claimed he was born a citizen (Acts 22:29), which probably means his father was granted citizenship by performing some service to the empire. Also, in this story Paul is portrayed as one who claimed his legal rights as a citizen. One of the rights of Roman citizenship was something similar to what is commonly described as "due process." Instead of letting the justice system formally convict him as a criminal deserving of punishment, the crowd had proceeded to beat or flog him before he was found guilty of anything. When the magistrates heard this was done to a citizen, they were alarmed. After apologizing to them, the authorities quietly escorted Paul and Silas from the prison and asked them to leave town. They did not want any more embarrassments. So, Paul left the city and headed south. He apparently passed through the towns of Amphipolis and Apollonia en route to Thessalonica. Incidentally, the "we" passages cease their appearance here and do not reappear until 20:5, when Paul returns to Philippi during his third journey.

Ministry in Thessalonica

The city of Thessalonica, named after the sister of Alexander the Great, was the capital city of the province of Macedonia. In reward for the city's loyalty to the emperor, Augustus granted Thessalonica the status of "free city." One of the special privileges this status provided was the right of self-government.

Luke indicates that Paul ministered in the synagogues over three Sabbaths and argued from the Scriptures that the Messiah must suffer, die, and rise again, and that Jesus is the Messiah. From what can be known from other texts, the word of the cross had become a stumbling block for many Jews (1 Cor 1:18–25); traditional Jewish messianic concepts only affirmed a triumphant Messiah, not one in apparent defeat. As a result, the text states that Paul converted a few (literally "some") Jews but many devout Greeks and prominent women. The writer does not explain why Paul seemingly had more success among the Gentiles than the Jews. Perhaps the fact that Paul did not require Gentiles to observe the ceremonial requirements of the Mosaic Law and was known to be a Roman citizen might have made him and his message more appealing and credible to a Gentile audience.

Opposition by the Jews

But, as with nearly every city Paul evangelized in, trouble rose up against him and his fellow workers. However, this time the actual troublemakers had been incited by Jewish opponents. The crowds of agitators first looked for Paul at the home of a certain Jason, who had been the host of Paul and his associates. Not finding him, they dragged Jason to stand before the local officials and charged him with supporting men who were troublemakers and disloyal to Rome because they defied the emperor's decrees by proclaiming Christ as king. Furthermore, they accused Paul and Silas with turning the world upside down, which probably means that they caused trouble in every town they visited. The reference to the decrees of the emperor apparently refer to Caesar's edicts that outlawed any action and/or word that could be interpreted as disloyal to Rome. Any hint of disloyalty allowed in Thessalonica could have meant risking the loss of its special status as a free city. The authorities forced Paul's host, Jason, to pay a bond or fine, and Paul and his associates left the city earlier than they had planned.

Ministry in Berea

After being forced to leave Thessalonica, Paul went to the city of Berea and, as was his custom, he preached in the synagogue there. Interestingly, Acts describes the Jews in Berea as more noble and receptive than those in Thessalonica because they were willing to listen to Paul and examine Scripture to see if Paul was right. The result was that many Jews and Gentiles were converted. However, Jews from Thessalonica traveled to Berea and incited the crowd against Paul and forced him to leave. Nevertheless, Silas and Timothy stayed behind in Berea while Paul went on to Athens. The stories of Paul's evangelism in Thessalonica and Berea (and to some extent Philippi) highlight the theme that trouble was often associated with Christians but instigated by unbelievers, whether Jewish or Gentile.

For Further Study

Important Names and Terms

- Silas
- Timothy
- Bithynia
- Troas
- Lydia
- Pythoma
- Apollonia
- Jason

Questions

1. In your opinion, was it a good or bad thing that Paul and Barnabas broke up their missionary partnership? Explain.
2. Paul appealed to his Roman citizenship to point out injustice and demand an apology. Were his actions a result of feeling personally insulted, or did Paul have some higher purpose?
3. Paul was accused of being a threat to the social order. How were Paul and the Christian movement such a threat?

ACTS 17:16—18:21

Paul's Second Missionary Journey: Athens and Corinth

Special Topic: Cultural Setting in Athens

WHILE ATHENS WAS NOT quite the powerful city it had been during the zenith of the Greek empire, the city was still the center of culture in the ancient Greco-Roman world. If one wanted to study sculpture, literature, philosophy, and/or rhetoric, Athens was still the most attractive and influential city for these areas of studies. Athens was also a marketplace of ideas and religions, which is one of the reasons the city was full of idols, even to unknown gods. Luke states that Paul went both to the Jewish synagogue and the marketplace and preached in both locations. While in the marketplace, Paul found himself in dialogue and debate with Epicurean and Stoic philosophers.

Epicureanism-Pleasure the Chief End of Life

Epicureanism was founded by Epicurus, who lived 341–270 B.C. A simplistic description of Epicurean philosophy is that pleasure is regarded to be the chief end of life. However, pleasure in this sense should not be understood in some hedonistic or self-indulgent way. Rather, pleasure was understood as tranquility, associated with a freedom from pain or fear and enjoyment in the company of friends and loved ones. While Epicurus believed in the existence of the gods, he was a practical atheist, in the sense that the gods had no contact with or interest in humankind. The Epicureans believed that human existence is not the result of the will of some all-powerful deity, but of chance. And they taught there was no life after death—a belief that was understood to be a source of peace, since death meant there was a permanent end to pain and suffering. This view would have been in contrast with some of the popular views in the Hellenistic world about Hades.

Stoicism—Reason Is the Chief Goal of Life

The philosopher Zeno (340–265 B.C.) is usually credited with being the father of Stoic philosophy. The key to Stoicism seems to be reason. In contrast to Epicureanism, Stoics believed in God or the gods. The most important divine reality was sometimes called the *Logos*, a common Greek idea. The Logos was believed to be something like the universal spirit or mind, or even the soul of the universe. Thus, the divine was in all things, especially human beings. All humans were thought of as offspring of the Logos and each person was believed to have a spark of the divine within. The Stoics believed that one encounters or experiences the divine within through the use of the mind. Thus, Stoicism taught that humans are to live rationally and to control their emotions. Since the Logos is the soul of the universe, one must recognize that the Logos is in control, shaping and directing the cosmos to some ultimate purpose or goal. For one to live rationally as a Stoic, therefore, one must live according to the order of the cosmos. One must live in recognition of the divine order and purpose of everything in life. And since the gods or the Logos controls everything, humans must learn to live in personal resignation.

The Athenian philosophers apparently believed Paul was a propagator of some new religion that promoted different gods. Probably, they thought Paul's message of Jesus and the resurrection were the names of two deities: Jesus and *Anastasis*, the Greek word for resurrection.

Paul's Speech before the Areopagus

Since he was viewed as a propagator of a new philosophy or faith, Paul was brought before a council, called the Areopagus, to be heard and evaluated. The Areopagus consisted of respected and learned men who had the authority to examine all new teachings. The heart of Paul's speech centered on the identity and nature of the one and only true God of the universe. The springboard for the speech was Paul's acknowledgement of the many altars to various gods, including one to an unknown god. For Paul, this unknown god was the one true God he came to proclaim to them. His speech is the first extended address in Acts directed exclusively to a Greek audience. For that reason, there is no reference to the Old Testament prophets and how Jesus fulfilled the prophecies. In fact, neither the name Jesus nor even the idea of the promised Messiah of Israel are ever mentioned. There is a veiled reference to Jesus when he spoke of God judging the world in righteousness "by a man" (17:31) whom he raised from the dead, but his name is never given.

In his speech, Paul presented four major affirmations concerning the one and only true God:

1. The true God is the creator of all things. (He is sovereign.)
2. The true God needs nothing from this world. (He is self-sufficient).
3. The true God is not limited to shrines and temples. (He is infinite).
4. The true God is the creator of all human beings.

The affirmation of God as the creator of all things means that nothing in the universe is outside God's control and that everything owes its existence to God. While religions generally conceive of gods possessing powers beyond that of humans, most pagan religions did not understand the deity to be in absolute control or stand in supreme sovereignty over the created order. The gods of the Greek pantheon, though very powerful, seem be part of the cosmos. In fact, some groups, like the Epicureans, conceived of the gods as something like super-beings that were part of the material universe. But the God Paul proclaimed was supreme over all things.

A logical conclusion that comes from the belief that God is sovereign is that God is self-sufficient, needing nothing from human beings. Thus, what service one renders to God is done not because God needs it but because the human needs to serve God. Paul declared that the supreme and self- sufficient God gives to and blesses his creation, even human beings. The blessings on the creation might be in the form of rain and sunshine, which allow for plants and crops to grow and produce food for all living beings, including humans. Most importantly, God blesses humans with the gift of life itself and then sustains their lives with the provisions for life in nature. A God who nurtures his creation is not only self-sufficient, but also caring and loving.

Another aspect of God's supremacy is that he is not limited to sanctuaries or houses of worship, such as shrines and temples. God cannot be squeezed into a finite location for humans to honor and serve. Rather, God is infinite, i.e., God is not limited by time, knowledge, or space. Therefore, the God Paul proclaimed is greater than any deity the Greeks have ever believed in and the only one worthy to be served.

Finally, if God is the supreme creator of all things, including living beings, then every human being was created by this God. If this is true, then all humans have a common origin. Each person, therefore, is part of the human family through creation. And if all human beings are part of the same human family, then it should follow that this creator God cares for all humans equally and wants their best, especially for them to come into a renewed fellowship with him. As Paul expressed it, human beings were created for two reasons: (a) to inhabit the earth and (b) to seek after God. The story of creation in Genesis 1:27–30 emphasizes that human beings, both male and female, were created in the image of God. That special designation apparently includes a relationship with God. In other words, God created humans in his image in part to have fellowship with them. Paul then showed that even some of the leading Greek thinkers sensed this special connection between the deity and humans. He quoted from the Cretan philosopher Epimenides, who wrote, "In him we live and move and have our being," and the Stoic philosopher Aratus, who wrote, "For we too are his offspring." Even the Greeks understood that God is close to each person.

If God is the supreme infinite creator who needs nothing and yet cares deeply for his creation, of what value is idolatry? For Paul, idolatry is senseless since such a practice cannot adequately portray the infinite God.

For many generations, Paul said, God overlooked much of the false and inadequate methods to connect with and worship God, perhaps because these people had not received the formal Law of Moses. But with the arrival of Paul and his proclamation of this new faith, the times for ignorance were over. The time of repentance from a false faith to a true faith had come. Moreover, Paul stated that God will judge the world in righteousness (i.e., with justice) because all are to be judged by the man whom God appointed and later raised from the dead as proof of his divine appointment. The phrase "by a man" is the first and only reference in this speech to Jesus. Paul says that this man is to be the arm of God's judgment and that God had raised him from the dead as proof that God had appointed him.

Presumably, the judgment is to take place after this man dies and is raised, though nothing directly is said of the death of Jesus.

The results of Paul's speech were mixed: some scoffed or rejected it, and some were curious about this new teaching and wanted to hear more, including a certain Dionysius (who was a member of the Areopagus), a woman named Damaris, and some others who are unnamed. From that small group of interested persons, Paul was able to convince some to believe in Jesus. In my opinion, the majority of those who heard Paul's speech rejected his message primarily because some of Paul's convictions directly contradicted the prevailing Hellenistic worldview.

Special Topic: The Differences between the Gospel and Typical Ancient Greek Thought

The difference between the gospel and Greek thought is related to the differences of beliefs about God and the nature of the world and human beings. Drawing from its Old Testament roots, the Christian message taught that this universe is a creation of the supreme creator God, and that God made this universe to have a beginning and an end. The universe is not eternal, and history is moving like an arrow to an end—the end of all things, of this universe as we know it. When history reaches its end point, the plan of God will be fulfilled and judgment will commence to determine the eternal destiny of all humanity. Greeks, on the other hand, did not believe that history is moving to some end point; rather, it is never ending, always changing, but still remaining essentially the same with no ultimate goal for the universe.

As stated before, Christians believe that at the end of time all humans will be judged by God for the lives they have led. Obviously, since Greeks generally did not believe in some final end point to history, they also did not believe in the final universal judgment of creation.

Finally, Acts states that when the crowd heard about the resurrection of the dead, some of them scoffed. One of the most popular notions in the first century was the idea commonly labeled "dualism." By the first century, most versions of dualism looked at reality as consisting of two completely different realms: the physical and the spiritual. Generally speaking, dualism asserted that things associated with this physical world, including one's physical body, is bad or evil and certainly not meant for eternal happiness. Death, for Greeks, was the time when one escaped the limitations and evil of this physical life, which enables the soul to move on to purely spiritual realms. Though the Epicureans sometimes taught annihilation of the deceased after death, most Greeks believed in the immortality of the soul, i.e., the continued existence of something of their life force, but not one's personality or self-consciousness. In contrast, the gospel's belief in the resurrection of Jesus and hope for the resurrection of his people means that the body, though weak, is not inherently evil. And resurrection means that each person who is risen will continue to exist as a self-conscious being. This was the message of hope in the gospel that many of the Athenians rejected.

Ministry in Corinth

Paul departed Athens and traveled to the city of Corinth, in the provincial capital of Achaia (Greece). Corinth was a commercial power located on the southern peninsula of Achaia, known in ancient times as the Peloponnesus. At one time it had been the power of the old southern Greek empire, but the city had been destroyed by Rome in 144 B.C. as punishment for seeking its independence from Roman rule. Nearly a century later, Julius Caesar ordered that Corinth be rebuilt. Corinth eventually became a home for retired military officers, former slaves, and people from a variety of countries. Due to its favorable location for trade and the hard work of its citizenry, Corinth emerged from virtual extinction to become the wealthiest and most powerful city of the province.

When Paul arrived in Corinth, he stayed with Priscilla and Aquila, with whom he partnered in the trade of tent making, which can also refer to leather working in general. From his letters, Paul wrote that he rarely accepted money from the people he stayed with but rather supported himself by his trade. However, Paul may have ceased his "secular" job when Timothy and Silas arrived with news about the Macedonian churches. It seems that from then on he devoted all his energies to preaching the gospel.

The text indicates that Priscilla and Aquila had recently arrived from Rome after Emperor Claudius sent out an edict expelling all Jews from the city of Rome (probably around A.D. 49–50). The Roman historian Suetonius wrote that Claudius' edict of expulsion was precipitated by some kind of disturbance in the Jewish quarter concerning a certain "Chrestus" (Bruce, 347). Most likely "Chrestus" is a misspelling of the name "Christos," which is often translated "Christ" or "Messiah." This probably means that a disturbance arose involving Jewish believers in Christ, either as instigators or victims.

Paul's Second Missionary Journey: Athens and Corinth

As was his pattern, Paul first went to the synagogue and testified to his Jewish brethren concerning Jesus. He did this over several Sabbaths, but to little positive effect. Eventually, it was clear that the majority of the synagogue were opposed to his message. The opposition became so difficult that he decided to leave the synagogue and directly evangelize the Gentiles. In accordance with Jesus' instruction (Luke 9:4), Paul shook the dust off his clothes and went next door, where a Gentile God-fearer named Titius Justus welcomed him. It should not be overlooked that Paul chose to stay with a Gentile—a person who in most Jews' eyes was unclean as well as an unbeliever. Obviously, the gospel message that God is not a respecter of persons had been embraced by Paul. Ironically, Paul also converted one of the rulers of the synagogue, a certain Crispus, but it appears the bulk of his success was among the Gentile population. Paul even had a vision of Jesus exhorting him to stay in Corinth, which he did for about a year and a half.

The eighteen-month stay of Paul in Corinth took place during the administration of the proconsul Gallio, and since the proconsul generally served a one-year term, beginning and ending in the summer, it is often assumed that the Jewish leaders approached Gallio earlier on in his term, hoping he was not familiar with the conflict between the synagogue and the followers of Christ. The Jews charged Paul with introducing a new unauthorized religion. They may have implied that this new religion was a potential threat to Rome, but Gallio was unconvinced. He interpreted the dispute as simply a disagreement between two factions within Judaism and dismissed the case. Luke strangely mentions a certain Jew named Sosthenes, who was publicly beaten by the Jews without Gallio trying to stop it. It is uncertain whether Sosthenes was a Christian, though Paul referred to a Sosthenes at the beginning of his first letter to Corinth (1 Cor 1:1). If he was a Christian, Gallio was tacitly allowing the Jews to persecute believers in Jesus even though he ruled in favor of Paul. If Sosthenes was an unbelieving Jew, Gallio may have allowed fellow Jews to punish a brother for failing to win Paul's conviction. I think it is likely he was a Christian suffering persecution.

Additionally, Gallio's decision may have had the unintended consequences of providing legal protection for the church for the next two decades. Through the political maneuvering of Herod the Great, Rome granted the Jewish religion the legal status of "*Religio Licita*," i.e., it was a legally protected Religion within the Roman Empire. Gallio's ruling identified the Jesus movement as a sect of Judaism and thus entitled it to the same rights of legal protection as mainstream Judaism. These protections seem to have remained largely intact until the Jewish Wars and the destruction of Jerusalem, removing all legal protection for both the synagogue and the church.

Departure from Corinth

Paul had ministered in Corinth for eighteen months—the longest time he had spent in one place during his missionary journeys. At some point, Paul decided to return to Syria, specifically the church of Antioch of Syria, which had originally called him to the mission field. Apparently, Paul's plan was to sail from the port city of Cenchrea, which was very near Corinth. Nothing is said about how long Paul stayed in Cenchrea, but while he was there Paul shaved his head as part of a vow. This was probably the concluding ritual to the Nazarite vow (Num 6:1–21). Following the conclusion of the vow, he then sailed to Ephesus, the original goal of his second journey. Paul would only stay for a short time, but while there he "had a discussion" in the synagogue. When he decided to leave, Paul promised to return to Ephesus for a longer period, which he would do on his third and final missionary journey. The primary achievement of Paul's second missionary journey was the bringing of the gospel into Europe. Paul's third journey would concentrate on Roman Asia.

For Further Study

Important Names and Terms

- Epicureanism
- Stoicism
- Zeno
- Areopagus
- Epimenides

Questions

1. Based on Paul's speech, how does the attitude of hope make the Christian message different from Greek philosophy?
2. How does Paul's view of the true God suggest how humans beings are to live and treat each other?

ACTS 18:23—19:41

Paul's Third Missionary Journey: Ephesus

Survey of the Route of the Missionary Journey

FOLLOWING A BRIEF VISIT in Jerusalem, Paul went back to his supporting church in Antioch of Syria. Paul then left Antioch for his third journey. His travels took him through the province of Cilicia, where Paul's hometown of Tarsus was located. From Cilicia, the mission team moved through the provinces of Galatia and Phrygia, which included the towns of Derbe, Lystra, Iconium, and Antioch of Pisidia. Paul's journey continued through these provinces westward to the provincial capital of Ephesus, where he stayed for about three years (20:31). After he narrowly escaped a near riot in the city, Paul departed Ephesus and probably traveled through Troas to Macedonia, in particular the cities of Philippi, Thessalonica, and Berea. Paul's stay in those cities resulted in the establishment of Christian communities, but in each case his stay was cut short because of opposition and persecution. He left the province of Macedonia and went on to Achaia (Greece) and probably stayed in Corinth (and possibly Athens) for a period of three months. The return route was essentially a backtracking through Macedonia (Berea, Thessalonica, and Philippi) and Asia (Troas, Assos, Mitylene, Chios, Samos, Miletus, and Ephesus, where Paul met privately with the elders of the church). From Asia, Paul sailed to Tyre and traveled southward to Jerusalem.

Apollos in Ephesus (18:24–28)

Before Luke summarizes Paul's mission exploits, he introduces the reader to the preacher Apollos. The text seems to indicate that Apollos came to Ephesus shortly after Paul had left the city. It is not known whether Apollos had been carrying on an evangelistic tour and what other cities he may have visited; still, Luke's description is remarkably detailed. Apollos was a Jew and a native of Alexandria in Egypt. Alexandria was one of the major centers for Hellenistic (Greek) and Jewish philosophy and religion. It was in Alexandria that the Old Testament had been translated from Hebrew to Greek by the mid-second century B.C. Moreover, Alexandria had become a center for the allegorical reading of the Old Testament, a method that looks for deeper symbolic meaning of selected details of a text. Moreover, Apollos was apparently knowledgeable of the Scriptures, probably as a practitioner of the allegorical method of interpretation, along with an interest in prophecy fulfillment. Possibly, Apollos was influenced by Alexandria's eminent Jewish/Hellenistic theologian Philo. Luke also portrays Apollos as "eloquent" (18:24). This could mean he was trained in the Greek discipline of rhetoric.

Besides his Hellenistic/Jewish background, Apollos was at some level a follower of Jesus. The author says he was "instructed in the Way of the Lord "and "spoke with burning enthusiasm and taught accurately the things concerning Jesus" (18:25). The reference to "the Way of the Lord" may refer to the gospel proclaimed by the church or to the teachings of Jesus, and "the things concerning Jesus" could refer to information concerning the life and teachings of Jesus or the Old Testament prophecies concerning the coming of the Messiah. The text says that he taught with burning enthusiasm, which can refer to either general spiritual fervor or a fervor caused by the Holy Spirit.

According to Acts, Apollos knew only the baptism of John, which probably means he was a follower of the teachings of John the Baptist. Priscilla and Aquila instructed Apollos more accurately "the Way of God" (18:26), no doubt referring to the Christian gospel. While Apollos embraced a more accurate understanding of the gospel, nothing is said about whether or not Apollos was rebaptized, though the rebaptism of the twelve disciples of John in Acts 19:5 may suggest he was. From there, Apollos traveled on to Greece to strengthen the church. According to Acts 18:27–28, Apollos' primary contribution was in his interpretation of the Scriptures to publicly argue that Jesus was truly the Messiah of Israel. First Corinthians 1–4 shows that Apollos had made a significant impact in this Christian community. In fact, there may have emerged a group within the community that looked to Apollos as their spiritual leader.

Paul and the Disciples of John (19:1–7)

While Apollos was in Corinth, Paul found a group of men whom Acts labels "disciples." The word "disciples" is a term that in Luke/Acts normally means followers of Jesus. However, the word's meaning in this passage in difficult to determine. The word may also refer to believers on the fringe of Judaism, i.e., the Samaritans, or it could simply refer to a group of disciples of John the Baptist. Luke states that Paul asked the disciples if they had received the Holy Spirit when they became believers. In answer to Paul's question, these disciples indicated that they were not aware that there was a Holy Spirit. This does not mean these disciples had never heard of the existence of the Holy Spirit; rather, it means they did not know that the Holy Spirit had been poured out on God's people. Jews typically believed that the coming of the Messiah and the kingdom of God would include the gift of the Holy Spirit. Their ignorance concerning the Holy Spirit suggests they did not understand the gospel's affirmation of Jesus as Messiah and Lord.

Their answer to Paul's question about the Spirit apparently led Paul to ask them about their baptism. They replied that they knew only John's baptism. In response, Paul pointed out the difference between the baptism of John and the baptism of Jesus. Paul described John's baptism as a baptism of repentance that looks forward to the coming of the Messiah. In contrast, Christian baptism is in the name of Jesus, the Messiah. Thus, John's baptism was a baptism of anticipation while baptism into Christ was one of fulfillment.

Having become convinced of Paul's words, these disciples agreed to submit to baptism "in the name of the Lord Jesus" (19:5). Following their baptism, Paul laid his hands on them, after which the Holy Spirit fell on them and they began to speak in tongues and prophesy. This is the only example of rebaptism in Scripture, and it happened because the first baptism was not in the name of Jesus. Following their baptism, these disciples received the Holy Spirit by the laying on of Paul's hands. This is the third passage in which Acts portrays the Holy Spirit falling on believers followed by speaking in tongues and prophecy. The first text was the narrative concerning the day of Pentecost in Acts 2, and the second was the conversion of Cornelius the Roman centurion in Acts 10. It is also the third instance wherein someone lays hands on another after which the Holy Spirit is received. The first was the conversion of the Samaritans in Acts 8:14–17, and the second was the conversion of Saul of Tarsus in Acts 9:17–19. The laying on of hands was not only a way of dispensing the Spirit on someone but also of demonstrating acceptance by God and the Christian community. It appears that one of the literary strategies of Acts is to stress the importance of the universal nature of the gospel by highlighting the conversion of people or groups who occupied places on the cultural and religious margins. The dramatic coming of the Holy Spirit with the manifestations of tongues and prophecy would have been evidence that the new age of the kingdom had arrived, an age in which all people are invited to experience.

Paul's Teaching Ministry in Ephesus (19:8–10)

Paul had briefly visited Ephesus at the end of his second missionary journey and spent a little time reasoning with the members of the local synagogue. As he prepared to leave, he told them he would return to discuss the gospel with them. When he arrived in Ephesus during his third journey, the author states that Paul spent three months in the synagogue; this is considerably longer than the three weeks in Thessalonica. Yet, as in Thessalonica and Berea, there eventually arose strong opposition by the Jews, which forced Paul to leave the synagogue and look for another place to carry out his evangelistic work. The alternative venue was the Hall of Tyrannus. Paul was out of the synagogue and in the heart of the Greek world. The text states that he taught for two years in the Hall of Tyrannus. Since this place was probably used as a school during normal hours, Paul may have been allowed to use the facility in the afternoon when most would be resting from the Mediterranean heat (something like a siesta). Paul's classes could have been held from 1:00 to 4:00 p.m. The morning hours would have been a good time for Paul to carry out his tent-making trade. Luke states that the result of Paul's work in the Hall of Tyrannus was "that all the residents of Asia, both Jews and Greeks, heard the word of the Lord" (19:10). This brief statement suggests the possibility that Paul may have set up a training program to spread the gospel throughout Asia. Thus, Paul could have taught young men and women the gospel and sent them throughout the province of Asia Minor (or Roman Asia) to establish churches. This may explain the origin of the churches in Hierapolis, Laodicea, and Colossae. In fact, Paul suggested that he taught and sent out a certain Epaphras, who preached the gospel in Colossae, converted many people there, and established the church in that city (Col 1:3–8).

Paul and Evil Spirits (19:11–20)

One of the differences between evangelizing Gentiles and evangelizing Jews was the challenge of the occult. The practice of magic and the occult was widespread in ancient Rome and especially in the city of Ephesus. While in the synagogues, Paul concentrated on showing through Old Testament prophecy that Jesus was the Messiah, but among non-Jews Paul had to show something of the power of God in a world filled with demons, evil spirits, and fate. Through miracles (literally works of power) and exorcisms, Paul demonstrated that his God was greater than any god or evil power. He did this when he laid his hands on people and when they touched his handkerchiefs (or sweat rags) and found healing.

One example of the power of Jesus in Paul was in his encounter with the sons of Sceva. The sons of Sceva were itinerant self-proclaimed exorcists, who were more than likely charlatans seeking to take advantage of people's misery as they took their money ("son" here probably refers to a disciple). Nothing more is said of Sceva, but it is very unlikely that he was a genuine Jewish high priest. Probably the title "high priest" was a self-designation designed to enhance his standing among the people. These disciples of Sceva sought to cast out demons by the use of the name of Jesus. In the ancient world and even in some contemporary occult practices, it was believed that if someone knew a spirit's or demon's name, he could control it or gain access to its power. The use of Jesus' name by the sons of Sceva suggests that these believed Jesus to be a powerful spirit who could be used or manipulated to drive out evil spirits if the exorcist knew and spoke his name. When the sons of Sceva called on Jesus' name, the demon/evil spirit reacted by causing the possessed man to attack and strip these would-be exorcists of their clothing. The recognition of the power of Jesus in Paul was widely reported, which led to many converts who burned up their books on magic, witchcraft, and evil spells. Luke notes that the value of the books that were burned was about 50,000 silver coins (literally, "drachmas").

Conclusion

The story of Paul and the sons of Sceva provides a helpful window into the cultural world of the first century. Most people who lived in the first century believed that the world was filled with evil spirits and demons and lived in fear of being harmed by one or more spirits. As a result, many rituals were developed and performed in order to protect oneself from harm. The sons of Sceva did not believe in Jesus as the Son of God and Messiah, nor did they trust in his power, but they sought to gain access to control the power of Jesus in order to control or remove the evil demons and likely did so for selfish purposes. In contrast to these fears and obsessions with the demonic, the New Testament only rarely speaks of demons, and most of those references are found in the Gospels. Also, when the New Testament references them, it always affirms the power and authority of Jesus over all evil forces, thus giving people hope and confidence. Notice, too, that the power of Jesus in Paul to cast out spirits is accessed through faith in Jesus and not magic.

Demetrius and the Riot (19:23–41)

Demetrius was apparently a leader and organizer of a guild/union of artisans and craftsmen in Ephesus. Problems arose when it became apparent that Paul was making progress in persuading many to give up their worship of idols and place their faith in Jesus of Nazareth. In response to this, Demetrius accused Paul and the church with threatening the life and culture of Ephesus, including the worship of Artemis, the patron deity of Ephesus.

According to Greek myth, Artemis was the sister of Apollo and daughter of Zeus and Leto. She was regarded as the virgin huntress, the goddess of the wild. Worshippers thought of Artemis as the protector of chastity, the patroness of maidens of marriageable age. Outside of Greece, Artemis was regarded as the ancient mother goddess, the goddess of fertility, and associated with nature worship. Most likely, the Ephesians worshiped Artemis as the ancient mother goddess. The temple of Artemis was one of the Seven Wonders of the Ancient World.

In other words, Demetrius had sought to portray Paul as someone whose presence and beliefs threatened the very life of his community. However, it should also be noted that, as an artisan who had made his living from the sale of replicas of the goddess, Demetrius' motivations were also rooted in his loss of income from a decline in the sale of those figurines.

Paul's Third Missionary Journey: Ephesus

Demetrius' rhetoric was successful in turning the sentiment of many in the city against Paul. The angry mob went looking for Paul but instead found his host, Gaius, and Aristarchus, an associate of Paul. They dragged the two into the great amphitheater that was filled with an angry and nearly hysterical crowd. Most likely, this was not a legal hearing or assembly. According to Acts, the crowd was enraged; the city was filled with confusion and had rushed together into the theater, bringing people for questioning. Paul wanted to join his fellow believers in the amphitheater, but others would not let him go out of concern for his personal safety. Acts states there was also a Jew named Alexander who tried to present a defense before the crowd but was shouted down. He may have wanted either to support Paul's anti-idol position or, more likely, show that the local synagogue was not associated with Paul and his associates. It is worth noting that Luke states that when the crowd realized Alexander was a Jew, they began to shout him down also—a likely indication of anti-Semitic sentiments within the population at large.

For two hours, the crowd in near frenzy cheered, "Great is Artemis of the Ephesians." Recognizing the potential danger, the town clerk stepped in and quieted the crowd. In his speech, the clerk began by reaffirming the people's belief in the greatness of Artemis. He mentioned that the statue of Artemis had fallen from heaven. Perhaps this so-called statue was believed to be located in the temple. This statue has not been found, but it is thought it may have been a meteorite whose shape appeared to be the image of this multi-breasted mother goddess. Secondly, the clerk exonerated Paul and the Christians of any wrong or criminal action and that any formal complaint that Demetrius or anyone else might have against them must be handled in accordance with the law through the courts. Furthermore, he implied that Demetrius and others could be guilty of seeking to incite a riot. The town clerk did not want this incident to be prolonged or reported to his superiors. Rome was always very concerned about civil disorder and might punish an unruly city with the heavy arm of the Roman legion, which this clerk wanted to avoid. The clerk then released the Christians and dismissed the crowd, unknowingly signifying Roman recognition of Christianity as a legal and free religion. Most likely, Acts wants the reader to understand that God had been working behind the scenes in these events.

For Further Study

Important Names and Terms

- Apollos
- Philo
- Allegory
- Disciple
- Tyrannus
- Sceva
- Demetrius
- Artemis

Questions

1. Compare and contrast Paul's accomplishments in his second and third missionary journeys.
2. Identify the different religious and cultural groups in Ephesus Paul interacted with. How was the Christian gospel able to successfully minister to such different types of groups?
3. Identify one primary doctrine or idea in the Christian message that would be the most appealing to unbelievers from various backgrounds.

ACTS 20:1—21:16

Paul's Third Missionary Journey: Macedonia, Greece, and Return

Paul's Travel to Macedonia and Greece and Return to Troas (20:1–12)

AFTER THE CRISIS HAD passed, Paul left Ephesus and headed for Macedonia. While the timing of Paul's departure may have been influenced by the events incited by Demetrius, the idea of leaving Ephesus and the route Paul took had already been decided. According to Acts, Paul had indicated that he intended to travel through Macedonia and Achaia and then return to Jerusalem. Then, after spending some time in the city of David, Paul would set out on a journey to Rome (19:21–22). Most likely, after leaving Ephesus Paul spent some time in Macedonia, either Thessalonica or Philippi, where he wrote 2 Corinthians, and then went on to Greece and stayed there three months, during which time he wrote Romans. While Acts is silent about his intentions, it is likely that Paul's return journey to Jerusalem was for the purpose of delivering to the church the collection of money and other relief items for the poor in that region (Rom 15:23–33; 2 Cor 8–9).

According to 2 Corinthians 10–12, certain preachers who were opposed to Paul had arrived in Corinth and attacked Paul personally, questioning his authority as an apostle. While still in Macedonia, Paul wrote a stinging rebuke of these opponents and the church that had tolerated them. He also warned that if these troublemakers were still active in Corinth when he arrived, he would personally take matters into his hands by driving the troublemakers out of the church and disciplining those in the Corinthian church who supported them.

Paul then arrived in Greece (i.e., Corinth) and stayed for three months. At some point, Paul decided it was time to sail back to Syria, but news of a plot by certain Jewish opponents forced him to take the inland route through Berea, Thessalonica, Philippi, Neapolis, and Troas.

In Acts 20:6 the familiar "we" passage reappears ("*we* sailed from Philippi"). Previously, the pronoun "we" was used to apparently include the author (presumably, Luke)—most recently in 16:16–17 when Paul and company were in Philippi during the second missionary journey. Consequently, the phrase "we sailed from Philippi" appears to indicate that the author of Acts had been in Philippi since Paul's second missionary journey. Acts also states that the departure from Philippi during the third missionary journey took place "after the days of Unleavened Bread." Unleavened Bread was a weeklong festival that took place immediately after Passover. Thus Paul had planned his return to Jerusalem to take place during spring.

Troas

Paul's group arrived in Troas and stayed for a week, but Luke describes only the events of Sunday. According to Acts, the believers in Troas gathered on the first day of the week to break bread. The language may indicate that these believers gathered together for the expressed purpose of the breaking of bread. Most likely, Luke has in mind the Lord's Supper. This verse is one of only two places in the New Testament where the gathering of believers in Jesus took place on "the first day of the week" (see also 1 Cor 16:2). It is also likely that Sunday was assumed in the phrase "the Lord's day" (Rev 1:10). Evidence shows that by the second century Christians were meeting on the first day of the week, in contrast to the Jewish Sabbath and in honor of Jesus' resurrection on the first day of the week.

The Roman week did not contain or recognize a weekend break from work. People worked seven days a week, and the working class normally did not get off work until 6:00 p.m. In other words, church gatherings would have been evening events. For Paul to have spoken until midnight probably means he started sometime after six and continued until midnight. The Greek word suggests more of a dialogue or conversation than a lecture. Most likely, the room was crowded and stuffy from the lanterns and torches that gave light in the place. The long hours and warm stuffy conditions were too much for a young man named Eutychus, who, while sleeping, fell out of the window and apparently died. Paul assured the church that

Eutychus was okay and then proceeded to raise him from the dead. While some scholars have questioned whether Eutychus had really died or if Paul merely brought him back to consciousness, the context seems to require a resurrection miracle. Throughout Acts, the ministry of Paul is paralleled with that of Peter's. Here, Paul raised the boy in similar fashion to Peter's raising of Tabitha. After witnessing this miracle, the group of believers were encouraged in their faith.

Paul in Miletus (20:13-37)

After Paul left Troas, he traveled by ship to the coastal town of Assos, where he changed ships. From there he sailed to Mitylene, Chios, Samos, and then Miletus (all coastal towns, harbors, or islands). Paul had decided not to visit Ephesus or any other major place in Asia but to stay on the coast in order to not be delayed in arriving at Jerusalem by Pentecost. Yet, while staying in Miletus, he sent for the elders of the church in Ephesus to instruct them one last time.

Paul's Speech to the Elders

What has been preserved for the reader by Luke are instructions in the form of a farewell address. Near the end of Paul's instructions, he revealed his conviction that suffering and possibly death awaited him in Jerusalem. So, like Jesus who instructed the apostles in the upper room to prepare them for his absence, Paul gave his final instructions to these church leaders. First he declared that his own ministry among them was characterized by faithfulness and integrity. He reminded them how he served the Lord both in humility and in suffering through the opposition of others, particularly the Jews. Yet, through all his hardship, Paul contended he remained true to his calling and a preacher and teacher of the gospel. Nevertheless, he had become aware through the Holy Spirit that prison and hardship awaited him. Throughout Acts, there are three places where Paul's future suffering is either explicitly or implicitly discussed, and all three are in the context of his journey to Jerusalem (20:22–24; 21:4, 11–14). As Jesus had predicted his suffering in Jerusalem while on the road to the city, Paul did the same. It seems that Luke wants the reader to understand the suffering of Paul in light of the suffering of Jesus; he was a Christ-like sufferer. Also, the place of suffering for both Jesus and Paul was Jerusalem. Obviously, the big difference is that Jesus died in Jerusalem while Paul appealed to Rome and survived a few more years outside of Jerusalem. But Luke may have implied that, like Jesus, Paul's fate was sealed and that he was in fact dead by the time of the writing of Acts.

Paul's absence due to imprisonment and possibly death meant the Ephesian elders had to take on the responsibility of leading the church with greater seriousness. Paul believed this was particularly important because of the great spiritual challenges this church would face in the future. Paul predicted and warned the Ephesians elders of the coming of false teachers in their midst. Therefore, he exhorted the elders to faithfulness as shepherds of their spiritual flock. He instructed them to take stock of their own spiritual lives and be spiritually alert. He called them to be faithful in teaching the truth of the gospel and to faithfully refute the false teachers in order to protect the flock from their influence.

In 20:17, Luke records that Paul called for the elders of the church of Ephesus. Also, in verse 28, Paul said that the Holy Spirit made them overseers and that they were to "shepherd" (or "be shepherds over") the church of God. In these two verses Acts uses three important words to describe the leaders of the church: "elders," "overseers" (bishops), and "shepherds" (pastors). Each of these words conveys a certain quality of leadership. "Elder" suggests maturity and wisdom, "overseer" suggests leadership, and "shepherd" suggests qualities associated with nurture, care, and protection. In later centuries, each of these terms became names for separate church offices. Yet, originally these three words described the same ministry. It is also important to note that these terms originally were not intended as official titles but descriptions of what a leader does or is. He demonstrates wisdom, he is a good leader, and he cares about and for his people.

Paul was concerned about the future of the church, a community whose existence was paid for by the very sacrifice of Jesus. He died so that this community, this church, might exist and thrive. He knew that these false teachers would arise from within this Christian community and present attractive but dangerous temptations to change the spiritual direction and character of a church. He was also concerned about the future of the church because he knew he would not be there to personally guide, teach, and correct them. From then on, the elders had to take on that role.

Paul concluded with a prayer for God to keep them strong and close to him. Then, with tears, Paul said farewell to them and boarded a ship to sail to the destiny awaiting him. This farewell speech is significant to the narrative of Acts for three reasons: (1) it is the first instance of prophecy about Paul's imprisonment and suffering in Jerusalem; (2) it is the first instance of instructions on the responsibilities of church leaders; and (3) it is first instance of a warning and prediction of false teachers in the church.

Paul Returns Home (21:1-16)

After his emotional farewell to the Ephesian elders, Paul resumed his return trip to Jerusalem. The text mentions that he sailed a straight course by way of the islands Cos and Rhodes. From Rhodes he went to Patara, which is on the coast of Lycia, where he changed to a ship en route to Phoenicia. When the ship approached the island of Cyprus from the northwest, the captain piloted the vessel in a southeasterly direction past the island, so that it appeared, as Luke states, from the left. The ship finally docked in the Phoenician city of Tyre, and Paul stayed there seven days. During his stay in Tyre, Paul was warned "through the Spirit" (21:4) not to go to Jerusalem—no doubt referring to the message of unnamed prophets. But Paul was determined to complete his journey, so the believers escorted Paul and company to the harbor, where he said farewell and then returned to the ship.

Paul's next stop was Ptolemais. Located some forty miles south of Tyre, Ptolemais was the southernmost port of Phoenicia. After staying one night there, he proceeded an additional forty miles south to Caesarea. While there, Paul stayed at the home of Philip the Evangelist, the same Philip who evangelized in Samaria and baptized the Ethiopian (8:4–8, 26–40). According to Luke, Philip had four daughters (literally "virgins") who had the gift of prophecy. This is the first instance in Acts where specific women are identified as prophets, though Peter's quotation of the prophet Joel declared "and your sons and your daughters shall prophesy" (2:17b). According to church tradition, the religious order of "Virgin" originated with the daughters of Philip. While Philip's daughters seemed to be connected to a particular church, other prophets, like Agabus, seemed to be more like itinerant prophets, who moved about from one place to another as they sensed the movement of the Spirit. Earlier, Agabus appeared as the prophet of a future famine throughout the world, especially in Judea. As a result of his prophecy, Barnabas and Paul (known then as Saul) initiated a collection program in Antioch of Syria and brought those gifts to the poor in Jerusalem. Ironically, this same prophet appears as Paul apparently was bringing gifts from churches throughout the Roman world to help alleviate the suffering in Judea. Yet, this time his prophecy was not about a famine but about Paul's future arrest and imprisonment. Agabus took Paul's belt and tied Paul's hands and feet, and then said this would happen in Jerusalem to the one who owns the belt—i.e., Paul. Understandably, Paul's friends and associates tried to persuade Paul not to go to Jerusalem, yet Paul was determined to go and complete his mission even if that meant imprisonment and death.

For Further Study

Important Names and Terms

- Eutychus
- Miletus
- Pastor
- Bishop
- Ptolemais
- Patara

Questions

1. According to Paul's speech, what were the functions of the elders of the church, and is that similar or different from the function of church elders today?
2. Based on Acts' description of Philip the Evangelist's four daughters, along with other passages in Acts, what contribution(s) did women make to the ministry and growth of the church?

ACTS 21:18—28:31

The Arrest and Imprisonment of Paul

ACTS 21:17—23:11

The Arrest and Imprisonment of Paul in Jerusalem

Paul's Arrest in the Temple

When Paul and his company arrived in Jerusalem, they were welcomed by James and other representatives of the local Christian community. However, Paul's meeting with the Jerusalem leaders revealed serious challenges facing this apostle—challenges that bore some similarities with the those during the Jerusalem conference (15:1–35), but even more serious. The leader of the church, James, stated that there were reports that Paul was encouraging Jewish Christians to abandon the Mosaic Law and traditional Jewish practices. While there are no specifics in the narrative, it can reasonably be concluded that James was referring to Paul's refusal to require Gentile converts to observe circumcision, dietary restrictions, and Jewish purity codes. The author of Acts, however, is very clear that these charges were false. Paul faithfully attended synagogue services on the Sabbath (13:13–15, 44; 16:13; 17:1–2), observed a traditional Jewish vow (probably a Nazarite vow; 18:18–19), and even had young Timothy circumcised before Paul permitted him to minister to Jews in the synagogue (16:1–3). Yet, despite Paul's efforts to honor his Jewish heritage, the rumors persisted. So, James instructed Paul to demonstrate his respect for the Jewish Law by paying the expenses of men who were completing a vow (Num 6:13–18). In addition, James reiterated the earlier decision of the Jerusalem conference regarding Gentile believers' obligations towards the Mosaic Law.

After the required purity rituals had been performed by Paul and the other men, the text states that certain Asian Jews who had stirred up the crowd against Paul seized him and accused him of blasphemy. Specifically, the charges were:

> "Fellow Israelites, help! This is the man who is teaching everyone everywhere against our people, our law, and this place; more than that, he has actually brought Greeks into the temple and has defiled this holy place." (21:28)

These charges are remarkably similar to ones made against Stephen when Paul (or Saul) was a persecutor of the Jesus movement:

> "This man never stops saying things against this holy place and the law; [14] for we have heard him say that this Jesus of Nazareth will destroy this place and will change the customs that Moses handed on to us." (6:13–14)

Like Stephen, Paul was charged with speaking against the temple and rejecting the Law. Furthermore, Paul was also accused with defiling the temple by bringing Gentiles into the sacred space reserved only for Jews. In 1871, and then again in 1935, two first-century inscriptions that warned against unauthorized persons entering the temple area were found. The following is a translation of the Greek in Joseph Fitzmyer's commentary on Acts: "No one of another nation may enter within the fence and enclosure around the temple. Whoever is caught shall have himself to blame that his death ensues." (698) Luke, however, notes that Paul had not brought any Gentiles into the temple area, but rather an Asian Jew named Trophimus. Nevertheless, the inscription's warning helps explain the riot that broke out in the temple, with people trying to kill Paul. In a strange way, Paul, who had participated in the killing of Stephen, had become the object of people's murderous efforts—sort of a second Stephen. However, Paul's life was saved when a tribune (a commander of a Roman cohort) led a detachment of soldiers who broke up the rioters and arrested Paul. The mob continued to call for Paul's death, but the tribune protected him by having him carried away to a safe location. Paul, however, requested to speak to the crowd, but the tribune was concerned that would only increase the tension. According the text, the Roman asked Paul if he was the notorious Egyptian who stirred up a revolt with some four thousand assassins. The historian Josephus refers to this event in his *Jewish Wars*:

> But there was an Egyptian false prophet that did the Jews more mischief than the former; for he was a cheat, and pretended to be a prophet also, and got together thirty thousand men that were

The Arrest and Imprisonment of Paul in Jerusalem

> deluded by him; these he led roundabout from the wilderness to the mount which was called the Mount of Olives, and was ready to break into Jerusalem by force from that place; and if he could but once conquer the Roman garrison and the people, he intended to domineer over them by the assistance of those guards of his that were to break into the city with him. But Felix prevented his attempt, and met him with his Roman soldiers, while all the people assisted him in his attack upon them, insomuch that when it came to a battle, the Egyptian ran away, with a few others, while the greatest part of those that were with him were either destroyed or taken alive; but the rest of the multitude were dispersed everyone to their own homes, and there concealed themselves. (ii.13.5)

The fact that Josephus mentions the role of the Roman governor Felix—who was governor during 52–58/60, which includes Paul's imprisonment in Caesarea (57/58–59/60)—in putting down this revolt indicates that this was a recent event. Paul, however, simply identified himself as "a Jew, from Tarsus in Cilicia" (21:39). So, the tribune gave Paul permission to address the crowd. Paul motioned for their attention, the crowd quieted down, and he spoke to them in Aramaic. Literally, the text reads "in the Hebrew language" (21:40). No doubt, Paul's use of Aramaic would at least have let the people know that on some level he was one of them, a Jew.

In Acts there are three main defense speeches by Paul. The first is in 22:1–21, where Paul defended himself to the Jews who were assembled in the temple area. The second is an abbreviated defense before the Roman governor Felix (24:10–21). The third defense was before Herod Agrippa II and the governor Festus (26:1–29). In these three speeches, Paul defended himself before the Jewish crowd and three different governing officials. In all three speeches, Paul sought to describe and explain how and why he changed from being a persecutor of disciples of Jesus to a prominent preacher. He also stressed that his new faith in Jesus did not mean a complete rejection of his Hebrew faith and tradition. Rather, he believed his childhood faith found fulfillment in Messiah Jesus.

Paul's Defense before the Jews

Paul began his speech by reviewing his Jewish background. He asserted that he was born a Jew in Tarsus in Cilicia. Interestingly, only Acts identifies Tarsus as Paul's birthplace; nothing is mentioned of it in any of Paul's letters. This is also true concerning Paul's training under Gamaliel. The import of

Paul's words is that he had been brought to Jerusalem as a child, studied under the famous rabbi Gamaliel, and devoted his early life to serve God as a devout keeper of Torah. In other words, Paul was a Jew like his hearers. Furthermore, his devotion to God and Torah led him to persecute what he called "the Way." His role as a persecutor led him to arrest, bind, and imprison those who believed in Jesus. Not only did Paul persecute disciples of Jesus, he sought to arrest believers in distant cities such as Damascus. This led to a second version of Paul's account of his conversion. This version with a few variations is very similar to the version in 9:1–18. In both versions, there is the light from heaven; the voice saying "Saul, Saul, why are you persecuting me?"; the command to go to Damascus and wait for further instructions (with an additional comment in the second account that Paul's blindness was due to the brightness of the light); and mention of a certain Ananias, a strict observer of the Law, who both healed and baptized Paul.

Paul's version of his divine calling was deeply rooted in the Old Testament. First, Paul was called by the God of his ancestors (literally, "fathers"): the God of Abraham, Isaac, and Jacob. This God chose (elected) Paul to know God's will, see the righteous one (very similar to "righteous servant" in Isaiah 53:11), and hear his voice. All of this means that Paul received a prophetic calling, a calling with a mission to the whole world. God had called him to be his witness to all people, whether Jew or Gentile. The reference to the washing away of sin with baptism is similar to God forgiving and purifying Isaiah of his sins by touching his lips with a burning coal (Isa 6:6–8). Moral and spiritual purification prepared one for carrying out God's mission. Paul's speech also included another encounter with the risen Jesus, who commissioned him to leave Jerusalem and go away to the Gentiles in order to witness to them.

According to Acts, up to this point in the speech the crowd had listened to Paul. But when he mentioned a mission to associate with Gentiles, they became angry and called for his death. This is similar to the moment during Jesus' trial when the crowd began to shout, "Crucify him!" (Mark 15:13, 14; Luke 23:21; John 19:6, 15).

Recognizing that Paul had again angered the crowds with his words, the tribune directed that Paul be taken out and flogged in order to extract information from him concerning his identity and activities. Yet, before the flogging could be carried out, Paul raised the issue of the legality of flogging a Roman citizen. Roman citizenship was originally restricted to those who lived in the city of Rome. However, as the Roman Republic expanded into the Roman Empire, citizenship was extended to non-Romans as an award for services rendered to the empire. Citizenship was a mark of social distinction. Once conferred on a person who was head of a household, the status and rights of citizenship remained in the family of that person. When asked how he obtained his citizenship, Paul stated he was born a citizen, which means his father or grandfather must have been granted citizenship and it had passed on to Paul. It may be that Paul carried documents verifying his citizenship status. Nowhere in Paul's letters is there any mention of his Roman citizenship. However, Luke mentions Paul's Roman citizenship in three passages in Acts (16:37; 22:25; 25:11). In each case, the appeal of his Roman citizenship has to do with his rights as a prisoner. In 16:37 he protested of having been beaten and imprisoned without a fair trial. Here in 22:25, Paul appealed to his citizenship in order to avoid being flogged. Finally, in 25:11 Paul used his citizenship to appeal to Caesar and have his case transferred to Rome.

Paul before the Sanhedrin

When the tribune was convinced of Paul's citizenship, the tribune changed tactics by setting up a hearing before the Sanhedrin for the purpose of learning more about the controversy between Paul and the Jewish leadership. When the Jewish council had convened to interview Paul, the apostle declared before this group that his conscience was clear; he believed he had been faithfully doing God's will. In response to his words, the high priest, Ananias, ordered that Paul be struck on the mouth. Paul responded in angry rebuke by saying, "God will strike you, you whitewashed wall! Are you sitting there to judge me according to the law, and yet in violation of the law you order me to be struck?" (23:3). The phrase "God will strike" is sometimes used in the Old Testament as the language of a divine curse for disobedience (Deut 28:22). Paul's reference to whitewashed walls echo the words of Jesus in Matthew 23:27 that accused the high priest and his associates with overemphasis on outward appearance. Paul further charged Ananias with violating the Law in ordering Paul to be struck. Likely, Paul was referring to traditional legal principles, implied in texts such as Leviticus 19:15, which called for the protection of the accused during the trial. Some were shocked by Paul's words and asked him if he knew he was been speaking to the high priest. Paul answered by saying that he did not realize he had been speaking to the high priest. Yet, it is not clear from the text whether Paul really did not know who the high priest was or he was simply being sarcastic. However, it is possible that Paul did not know who the high priest, was since Ananias had been high priest from 47 to 59, essentially the years of Paul's missionary activity. According to contemporary historians, Ananias' tenure as high priest was marked by corruption, graft, and a decidedly pro-Roman policy.

Paul noticed there were both Sadducees and Pharisees present at the hearing. Consequently, as a defense strategy, he identified with the Pharisees, since they believed in resurrection. Paul charged that he was on trial because of his belief in resurrection. For Paul, this was not only a clever strategy; it was true because if Jesus had been raised from the dead, the claims of this Jesus' movement were true—that is, Jesus is the Messiah. The cleverness of Paul's strategy can be seen in the response of the Sanhedrin. His words caused a debate between the Sadducees and the Pharisees. Many of the Pharisees sided with Paul, even admitting the possibly that he had seen some kind of heavenly being. The disagreement grew intensely violent so that Paul had to be removed from the meeting with no resolution to this case. One interesting feature of this story is that even though Paul was the prisoner on trial, he was the one in control of the agenda of the meeting.

For Further Study

Important Names and Terms

- Trophimus
- Felix
- Festus
- Tarsus
- Flogging
- Torah

Questions

1. Why were the Jewish opponents so passionately against Paul and his message?
2. In Acts the apostles emphasize the resurrection of Jesus much more that his crucifixion. Why do you think this is so?

ACTS 23:12—26:32

The Imprisonment of Paul in Caesarea

Paul's Removal to Caesarea (23:12–35)

THE NIGHT AFTER PAUL returned to his cell, Luke states that the Lord stood near Paul and spoke to him. Acts mentions at least five appearances of Jesus to Paul:

1. On the Damascus road, which led to Paul's conversion (9:4)
2. In Troas, where he received the "Macedonian call" (16:9)
3. In Corinth, during his second missionary journey (18:9)
4. In the Jerusalem temple, shortly after his conversion but first mentioned during his defense speech to the Jews (23:11)
5. In the Jerusalem prison (23:11)

The words of Jesus during these meetings were either words of comfort in times of trial or commission to a new ministry. During Paul's Jerusalem encounter with Christ, Paul learned that he must testify in Rome. This is the first time that Rome is mentioned as Paul's ultimate destination as a prisoner for the Lord.

The Plot to Kill Paul

While the Roman authorities had been successful thus far in protecting Paul from harm, his enemies would not rest until he was killed. According to the text, some forty men took a vow to fast until Paul was killed. Their plan involved an ambush wherein Paul would be brought again to the Sanhedrin presumably for further questioning, only to be attacked by surprise and killed. Since they planned this with the knowledge of the chief priests and elders, one can only assume that at least most of the Sanhedrin was complicit in this murderous plot. However, fortunately or providentially, this plot was discovered by Paul's nephew. Paul instructed his nephew to report the plot to the tribune, who, after being convinced of the plot's likelihood, decided to secretly remove Paul to Caesarea. The swift nature of the decision to remove Paul shows how seriously the tribune considered the threat. The transfer company left at 9:00 p.m. and included two hundred soldiers, seventy horsemen, and two hundred spearmen. If these numbers are taken literally, then one can only assume that the tribune considered the protection of Paul a high priority. The large number of soldiers may also indicate that the Romans regarded the forty or more conspirators to be very dangerous and required overwhelming force to defeat them, or that since Paul was a Roman citizen it was extremely important to insure his safety.

The leader of this prison escort was a centurion, Claudius Lysias. Acts records portions of a letter sent to Governor Felix from Claudius Lysias explaining the reason for transferring Paul to Caesarea. The details in the letter are consistent with those in Luke's narrative. One significant difference is that Claudius claimed that the reason he rescued Paul from the violent mob in the temple was that he learned Paul was a Roman citizen—no doubt embellishing his own record before his superior. When Paul arrived in Caesarea, Felix read the letter from Claudius Lysias and agreed to hear from Paul, but only after his accusers had arrived from Jerusalem. Meanwhile, Paul was to be kept under guard.

Paul before Felix (24:1–27)

Five days after Paul's transfer to Caesarea, the representatives from Jerusalem and the high priest arrived with legal charges against Paul. The spokesman for the accusers was a lawyer named Tertullus. This was a very common name throughout the Graeco-Roman world, so the person could have been either a Hellenistic Jew or a Gentile hired to represent these Jews. Tertullus brought before Felix a threefold charge against Paul: (1) Paul was accused of being a troublemaker, i.e., a dangerous insurrectionist. Presumably the evidence for this was that in every city where Paul visited and taught, there were disturbances and even riots. (2) Paul was accused of being the "ringleader" of an extremist sect of the Nazarenes. The word "sect" implies that the Jesus movement was considered a heretical branch of Judaism. Perhaps Tertullus' rhetoric suggests that Paul and his fellow believers did not represent mainstream Judaism. This is the only place in the New Testament where "the Nazarenes" was used to refer to disciples of Jesus. (3) Paul was accused of trying to desecrate the temple of Jerusalem. Tertullus portrayed Paul as one who had no respect for traditional Jewish practices or traditions.

After Tertullus completed his case against Paul, Felix allowed Paul to respond. Paul began by emphatically denying that he was a troublemaker or a defiler of the temple. He also asserted that his accusers had no evidence for their charges. In Paul's rejection of these charges, he came very close to accusing the temple authorities with bearing false witness. Most of Paul's defense focused on his religious beliefs and teachings. Interestingly, Paul's defense did not mention Jesus by name and only alluded to the gospel message with a reference to resurrection. Paul affirmed that he worshipped "the God of our ancestors" (24:14)—the God of Israel—and that he continued to believe everything laid down according to the Law and the Prophets. Furthermore, Paul affirmed his faith in the resurrection of the righteous and the unrighteous. By saying these things, Paul again was clearly siding with the Pharisees in contrast with the Sadducees. In Paul's mind, the real troublemakers were the Jews from Asia, not Paul or others believers of Jesus. These Jews from Asia were the ones who had stirred up the crowd in the temple and made the false accusation about desecrating the temple. Throughout Acts, Luke portrays the church as a victim of violent disturbances, not the cause of them. Paul's defense concluded by pointing to the belief in the resurrection from the dead as the real issue for why he was arrested and put on trial. The Sadducees rejected resurrection, while the Pharisees accepted it, although not the claim concerning Jesus' resurrection. Paul's belief in Jesus as the Messiah rested on the claim that he rose from the dead. If Jesus had been raised from the dead, everything had been changed.

On a side note, Paul's reference to bringing alms to his nation and offering sacrifices is often identified with the collection of money Paul collected from churches in Achaia, Macedonia, and Asia to the Jerusalem church for the relief of the poor (1 Cor 16:1–4; 2 Cor 8–9; Rom 15:23–29).

After hearing from the plaintiffs and the defense, Governor Felix decided to delay making a decision and hold Paul in custody. It is not clear what Felix's motives for his decision were. He may have been privately sympathetic to Paul but decided not to release him in order to protect him from the ongoing conspiracy against his life. The fact that he allowed Paul more freedom during his house arrest supports that theory. It could also be that Felix wanted to go out of his way to treat Paul well, knowing he was a Roman citizen. In addition, Acts notes that Felix and his wife, Drusilla, continued to meet privately with Paul. The text also indicates that Paul discussed with them faith in Christ: apparently they were wanting to know more about Jesus and the gospel message. Paul also talked about justice, self-control, and future judgment. For some reason, when Paul began speaking on these subjects, Felix became frightened and stopped meeting with him. Apparently Paul's moral demands were too much for Felix and Drusilla. For example, Drusilla (a Jewess) may have been enticed to leave her first husband and marry Felix; perhaps Paul's message condemned them for their sinful union. This echoes of Herod Antipas and Herodias (Mark 6:17–29; Luke 3:18–20; 9:7–9). Furthermore, it is possible that Felix believed Paul was rich or had access to wealth since Felix hinted that he would release Paul if the bribe was the right amount. Yet no bribe was ever offered. Paul remained in custody for two years until Porcius Festus replaced Felix as the new procurator/governor.

Paul before Festus (25:1–27)

Porcius Festus succeeded Felix in 58–60 and left office in 62. In contrast to Felix, Festus was a secular Roman who was unfamiliar with the beliefs of Jews and Christians. Thus, after the new procurator took office and made an introductory visit to Jerusalem, the temple leadership decided to resubmit their charges against Paul. Most likely they believed that the new uninformed government administrator would simply rely on their claims and release Paul to be tried in Jerusalem. However, Luke suggests that their request to Festus had not been made out of a desire for Roman justice but rather as a ploy to assassinate Paul. While unaware of this plot, Festus' first response was to insist that Paul be tried at the capital of Caesarea. Sometime later, he appeared to be agreeable to their request. After staying a little over a week in Jerusalem, Festus returned to Caesarea and sent for Paul. At this meeting with Paul, the governor proposed for Paul to be tried in front of his peers in Jerusalem, the city where he was arrested, which may have seemed to be a reasonable alternative to a trial in Caesarea before an unsympathetic Roman judge. Much to the governor's surprise, however, Paul not only rejected this proposal but instead appealed to the emperor.

Before he appealed to the emperor, Paul made a brief personal defense to Festus. First, he stated that he did not violate the Law of the Jews. Also, he said he did not violate the sanctity of the temple or the laws of Caesar. By appealing to the emperor, Paul invoked his right as a Roman citizen, and such a right could be not ignored. Paul was fully aware that if he agreed to go to Jerusalem to be tried, he most likely would be killed. Consequently, Paul found a way to both escape the assassination plot and also fulfill God's plan for him to testify in Rome. Therefore, Festus had no choice but to accept Paul's appeal and send him to Rome. Yet, what charges would Paul appeal? Festus understood the controversy as purely religious. He did not believe Paul was guilty of any civil crime, and as a skeptical Roman he regarded the Jewish religion as mere superstition. Yet, despite his secular attitude, he did understand that one of the central points of disagreement between Jews and Christ followers was the claim that Jesus had been raised from the dead. Festus was not sure what to do, so he sought out advice from Herod Agrippa II (Luke simply calls him "Agrippa"). Festus reviewed Paul's case to Agrippa, who would have been somewhat familiar with the controversy between Jews and the followers of Jesus. Agrippa agreed to hear from Paul.

Paul before Agrippa (26:1–32)

Herod Agrippa II, the last of the line of Herod to possess political and governmental power, was the son of Herod Agrippa I (12:1–11, 20–23), the one who killed James and imprisoned Peter and, according to Acts, was struck dead by an angel. Agrippa II was born in 27 and educated in Rome. He was the brother of both Bernice, the future wife of Emperor Titus, and Drusilla, the wife of Festus' predecessor, Felix. The scene in Acts 25:23–27 somewhat sarcastically shows the stark contrast between the lavish ceremony associated with the entrance of Agrippa and Bernice into the hall, which, according to Luke, included "military tribunes and the prominent men of the city," and the lone prisoner, Paul. All the physical symbols point to Paul being in a position of considerable vulnerability, but again Paul took control of the moment.

Paul's Speech before Agrippa

After Agrippa gave Paul permission to speak, the apostle proceeded to summarize his Jewish background. According to Luke's account, Paul did not mention his hometown of Tarsus. Rather, he began by noting that he had been brought up in Jerusalem and that this was common knowledge. It was also widely known that he formerly lived as a Pharisee, which he described as "the strictest sect of our religion" (26:5). Note that he characterized Judaism as "our religion," which suggests that Paul believed that his faith in Jesus was not a complete repudiation of his Jewish faith. In fact, Paul argued that he was on trial because of his Jewish faith, or, as he stated it: "I stand here on trial on account of my hope in the promise made by God to our ancestors, a promise that our twelve tribes hope to attain, as they earnestly worship day and night. It is for this hope, your Excellency, that I am accused by Jews" (26:6–7). The key word for Paul here is "hope." The word "hope" appears eight times in Acts, of which five are associated with Paul's defense speeches (23:6; 24:15; 26:6–7; 28:20). The significance of the word "hope" is that it implies continuity between the past, present, and future (i.e., what was promised and hoped for in the past finds fulfillment in either the present or future work of God). The point is that Paul argued that he was on trial for believing and preaching the hope of Israel. Paul believed that the gospel, especially the resurrection of Jesus, fulfilled the hopes of ancient Israel. For Paul, the crux of the matter is the belief that God has and will raise the dead.

Paul also told Agrippa that prior to his encounter with the living Jesus, he had vigorously opposed this messianic movement. As an early persecutor, Paul admitted that he made several arrests and imprisonments and consented to the death of more than one Christian. But then his life was dramatically and permanently altered. The vigorous and committed persecutor became a courageous advocate for Jesus and his way. This is the third and final version of Paul's encounter with the risen Jesus. In this version, there is considerable emphasis on the light, but no mention of Paul's blindness resulting from the light. The text notes that the voice spoke in Hebrew or Aramaic—the voice from the heritage of Israel. In addition to asking Paul why he was persecuting him, this third version adds that the voice also said, "It hurts you to kick against the goads" (26:14). (A "goad" was some kind of long stick used to goad or prick an animal to get it to move. The voice was saying that, like a stubborn donkey that resists the prodding of the goads, Paul had been resisting the call of God.) Consequently this version is more a story of divine calling than of conversion. There is no mention of Paul's baptism or the role of the preacher Ananias who laid hands on him, healed him, and baptized him. Instead, the story is similar to the calling of the prophets Jeremiah and Isaiah. The risen Jesus appeared to him and called him to be a witness to both Jews and Gentiles. His calling included bringing a message of repentance (turning people from darkness to light), mercy (that people receive forgiveness of sins), and hope (that they might have a place among the sanctified).

Paul described his encounter with the risen Jesus as a "heavenly vision" (26:19), an experience that transformed him into a witness on behalf of Jesus. His calling/conversion led him to testify "in Damascus, then in Jerusalem and throughout the countryside of Judea, and also to the Gentiles" (26:20); this echoes Jesus' commission of the Twelve in 1:8. Like John the Baptist before him (Luke 3:17–19), Paul preached a message that called people to repentance and to perform deeds worthy of repentance. In contrast to the previous two versions of Paul's conversion, Paul stated here that the Jewish opposition was like their ancestors' opposition to the prophets. Paul, like the prophets before him, was calling Israel to genuine repentance, and "for this reason" his opponents had been trying to kill him (see Stephen's words to the Sanhedrin in 7:51–53). And yet, Paul's message was really the message of the Old Testament prophets concerning the Messiah in regards to his death, resurrection, and mission to Gentiles. The implication of Paul's words is that the temple authorities' opposition to him was really an opposition to God and his plan.

Festus responded to Paul's remarks by immediately dismissing Paul's testimony and calling him crazy. No doubt, Festus' attitude typified the religious skepticism associated with Roman culture. Paul quickly rejected Festus' interpretation and strongly insisted that he was speaking the truth. Then Paul appealed to Agrippa and his knowledge of the prophets. Paul may have only wanted to get Agrippa to say that he was in continuity with the prophetic tradition and that being a Jewish prophet was not a crime. Agrippa sarcastically dodged the question by suggesting that Paul wanted to convert him. There are several different versions of Acts 26:28. Below are four that are representative of the translation tradition of this verse:

1. "Almost thou persuadest me to be a Christian" (KJV).
2. "In a short time you will persuade me to become a Christian" (NASB).
3. "Are you so quickly persuading me to become a Christian?" (NRSV).

4. "Do you think that in such a short time you can persuade me to be a Christian?" (NIV).

Either Agrippa was sarcastically ridiculing Paul for thinking he could convert him or he was acting playfully with Paul, referring to converting to Jesus as ludicrous or a joke. The point is that Agrippa really was not near to believing in Christ, nor was he even sympathetic with Paul. Not surprised by Agrippa's response, Paul simply stated his profound desire that all people, including Agrippa, would come to faith in Jesus.

Conclusion

When Paul had finished, the meeting was over and everyone began exiting the hall. There had been no public verdict or even a stated opinion. Yet, privately, Agrippa, Bernice, and Festus all agreed Paul was not guilty of any crime and should have been released if it were not for Paul's appeal to Rome. To release Paul after he had appealed to the emperor would be to publically offend the authority of the emperor. Festus and Agrippa did not want to do that. Paul's appeal to the emperor had to be honored. Thus, Festus made arrangements for Paul to be sent to Rome.

For Further Study

Important Names and Terms

- Claudius Lysias
- Tertullus
- Drusilla
- Agrippa
- Bernice
- Goads

The Imprisonment of Paul in Caesarea

Questions

1. Reread the three versions of Paul's conversion to Christ (9:1–22; 22:4–16; 24:9–18) and note common elements among all three. What are the unique items in each version?

2. Some scholars have compared the trial experience of Paul in Acts to that of Jesus in Luke 22:66—23:25. Compare and contrast Paul's trial stories with those of Jesus in Luke. Is it possible the story of Paul's trials was shaped from the story of Jesus' trials?

3. What was Paul's attitude toward the Jewish religion?

ACTS 27–28

Paul's Voyage to Rome

Introduction

WHEN IT WAS TIME to set sail for Rome, Paul, some other prisoners, and a few of his companions were put onboard a merchant vessel. While Rome was the most powerful military in the known world, she was not regarded as a sea power. Consequently, there were no military naval transports or passenger ships except perhaps in times of war. Thus military personnel, like the centurion Julius, would typically contract with a private commercial vessel to transport people. Commercial vessels usually sailed near land, and the time that a vessel would venture onto the high seas was during the warmer months of the year since the fall and winter months were regarded as a dangerous time for sailing. From about November 11 to March 10, the Mediterranean was usually regarded as closed for travel (*mare clausam*, which means "closed sea") due to the dangerous conditions. Sometimes the sea was regarded as closed as early as October. Yet, according to Acts, Paul and his group set sail sometime after "the Fast" (27:9), a reference to the Day of Atonement, which takes place in the fall (late September to mid October). The significance of this is that Paul and company set sail during a time that was generally regarded as risky if not dangerous. This perilous situation would become even more acute when the ship was caught in the middle of a dangerous storm.

Paul's Voyage to Rome

The Voyage Begins (27:1–8)

As noted above, the military authority in charge of prisoners was Julius, a centurion of the Augustan cohort. The Augustan cohort was one of the five cohorts stationed at or near the provincial capital of Caesarea and largely consisted of Syrian mercenaries. Paul and company boarded a ship from the town of Adramyttium, an important coastal town on the northwest coast of Asia Minor. Based on Luke's description of the vessel's route, this ship likely was a "coaster"—a trading vessel hugging the coastline. In 27:2 the text reads "we put to sea"; the first-person "we" seems to indicate the author was with Paul on the ship.

After the ship departed from Caesarea, they sailed to Phoenicia and landed at the ancient city of Sidon. While they were in port, the centurion allowed Paul to visit some friends—a very generous gesture. When Paul's ship left Sidon, it sailed for the coastal town of Myra. Luke notes that the ship "sailed under the lee of Cyprus," meaning the eastern side of Cyprus, which provided some protection from the strong headwinds. Once they sailed safely around Cyprus, they proceeded northwesterly toward the coast of Asia Minor until they arrived at Myra on the southern coast of Asia Minor. In Myra, Julius the centurion found a ship from Alexandria, Egypt, that was bound for Italy and transferred the prisoners to that ship. Apparently there had been no ships scheduled to sail from Caesarea to Rome, so Julius had to first sail to another location (Myra) where he, along with the rest of the passengers, could transfer to a ship going to Rome. It is not surprising that Julius found transportation to Rome on a ship that originated in Alexandria. Ships from Alexandria typically carried grain and other freight from Egypt to Rome. The historian Suetonius stated that Emperor Claudius ordered that grain be shipped directly to Rome even during the winter. This Alexandrian ship with its new passengers departed Myra and sailed toward the island of Crete. The journey started slowly and after several days of difficult sailing arrived off the coast of Cnidus, a peninsula on the southwest tip of Asia Minor between the islands of Cos and Rhodes. Facing strong headwinds, they sailed under the lee (eastern protective side) of Crete, opposite Salmone. They continued sailing in a southwesterly direction to the small and obscure port of Fair Havens, near the equally obscure city of Lasea.

Preparation for Second Part of the Voyage (27:9–12)

Up to this point, the voyage had gone according to plan. The group departed Caesarea and sailed to Myra, where they transferred to a ship from Alexandria headed for Italy. There had been no problems, which was remarkable considering they were sailing at a potentially dangerous time of the year. But everything was about to dramatically change. Since he was a prophet, Paul knew (or sensed) that danger was a real possibility, so he warned the centurion that disaster awaited them if they continued sailing and did not wait until winter was over. This is the first of four times that Paul, a prisoner, intervened and gave advice or instruction to the ship's crew or centurion. But Paul's warning was rejected, and both the ship's pilot and its owner expressed confidence that they could safely make it to Italy. This would be the last time Paul would be ignored by those supposedly in charge. The captain decided to continue sailing westward for Phoenix, a town farther to the west on the southern coast of Crete. The captain wanted to reach Phoenix because it had a better harbor than Fair Havens and would be a more favorable location for spending the winter.

The Storm (27:13–20)

Initially, the weather conditions seemed to favor the captain's decision to sail on to Phoenix. Then, suddenly and unexpectedly, the ship was hit with strong winds from the northwest, commonly known as a "northeaster." The winds were too strong for the ship to resist and sail through, so the captain decided to give way to the force of the winds and allow it to drive the ship southward away from Crete. Eventually the ship came near the lee of a tiny island called Cauda, located about twenty to thirty miles south-southwest of Phoenix. With minimal protection from the island, the crew sought to prepare the ship for even rougher wind and sea conditions. Luke states that due to the weather the crew had been "scarcely able to get the ship's boat under control" (27:16). With great difficulty they were able to secure the dinghy and keep it from slamming into the ship's hull.

The crew also had to "undergird the ship," i.e., run cables under and over the hull to keep the ship from breaking up. As conditions continued to worsen, the captain ordered that the crew lower the anchors to slow the ship's movements in order to avoid running into a reef or the sandbars off the northern coast of Africa, known as "the Syrtis." However, when the storm continued to threaten the ship and crew, it was decided to throw the cargo and ship's tackle overboard to lighten ship in order to ride out the storm more easily. With no end of the storm in sight and neither sun nor stars for navigation due to the heavy clouds, Luke states they appeared hopelessly lost.

Paul's Second Speech—a Speech of Assurance (27:21-26)

In the midst of their hopelessness and desperate situation, Paul spoke a word of encouragement to crew and passengers alike. First he reminded them that if they had listened to him early on, all this difficulty could have been avoided; this was sort of the "I told you so" part of the speech. Yet, despite these errors in judgment, Paul assured them that they would survive the ordeal. Paul could assure them because God, through an angel, had assured him that he must stand before Caesar and that God would also keep safe all those who had been traveling with him, both crew members and fellow passengers. Having given this encouraging message, Paul warned them that the danger was not yet over and that their ship would have to run aground near some island.

Paul explicitly declared that it was God's will to get Paul to Rome. However, if God wanted Paul to get to Rome, then why would he allow the storm to occur? One explanation is that Luke wants the reader to see how God often overrules human mistakes in order to accomplish his will. A second explanation is that the writer wants to show God as sovereign over the created order (the creator is more powerful than the creation). A third possible explanation, and the one this writer believes is most likely, is that Luke interpreted the storm as the instrument of the forces of darkness that were attacking Paul and trying to prevent Paul from fulfilling God's plan for him in Rome. God's intervention and ultimate deliverance of Paul and the rest testifies to God's sovereignty over all the forces of the devil who seek to thwart God's eternal plan. Luke's message is that nothing can stop God in the accomplishing of his will for creation.

Discovery of Land (27:27-38)

Two weeks after the storm hit the ship (or as Acts expresses it, "On the fourteenth night"; 27:27), the crew began to sense that they were nearing land. For several days they had been drifting across the sea of Adria, the sea between Crete, North Africa, Greece, and Sicily. In order to test the crew's suspicions about land, they proceeded to take soundings at different depths. Probably using a rope with some type of weighted object attached to one end, they dropped the line and learned that the water's depth was 20 fathoms, or 120 feet. Sometime later a second sounding was taken and the results were 15 fathoms, or 90 feet. The more shallow water was a good sign that land was near. The crew lowered the ship's anchor to slow the ship's movement and prevent running aground, waiting for and praying for morning to come.

As this was going on, some of the men, apparently in a state of panic and desperation and fearing the ship would crash into the rocks, attempted to abandon the ship by taking the lifeboats. In true leadership fashion, Paul assessed the crisis and told the soldiers that all must be aboard if any were to be saved. Paul understood that the desperate men's actions could easily incite more escape attempts, putting everyone's life at risk. Everyone would be needed to help save the boat and its passengers. So, the boats were cut away to prevent all escape attempts.

In another act of leadership, Paul encouraged people to eat to keep up their strength. He assured both the crew and the passengers that they would all survive the crisis. After this, Paul offered grace for the food and had it distributed to all the people. The text reads that Paul "took bread; and giving thanks to God in the presence of all, he broke it and began to eat" (27:35). This scene is not unlike a typical Jewish meal, which always begins with grace. The words in the narrative are very similar to the story of Jesus' feeding the five thousand and even the Last Supper. The story may have most in common with Jesus' feeding of the five thousand. Paul's words and actions are roughly similar to the actions and words of Jesus. In both settings, the people who ate were people who were hungry. Also, Luke notes that everyone ate. Finally, the story carefully notes that there were 276 people on the ship who were fed. After they had finished eating, the people threw the rest of the wheat overboard to further lighten the ship.

Landing on Malta (27:39–44)

In the morning, the sailors sighted land that was unfamiliar to them. They also sighted a bay with a beach. The traditional site for the landing of Paul and the crew is located on the northeast coast of the island of Malta and is called St. Paul's Bay. When they saw the bay and beach, they headed for land. The sailors cut loose the anchors, loosened the rope that tied the steering oars, and unfurled the sail in order that the wind might drive them onto the beach. Yet, despite these prudent and appropriate actions, they encountered trouble: the ship struck a sandbar and ran aground. The text reads that the ship struck "a reef" (27:41). The Greek word for "reef" literally means "a place of two (cross-) seas." This could mean that the ship hit a strait or sandbar that seemed to be a dividing place in the sea. The word could also refer to a shallow stretch of water caused by strong crosswinds. In any case, the ship ran aground, and its bow became stuck and immovable. Even worse, the force of the waves was beginning to break up the stern, effectively destroying the ship.

As the ship was breaking apart, people began to abandon it and make for shore. Not surprisingly, the prisoners could see this as an opportunity to escape. For that reason, it was a common practice for prison guards to execute prisoners in this kind of a situation in order to prevent their flight to freedom. Yet Julius the centurion, in order to keep Paul safe, prevented the guards from carrying out such a plan. Despite the extreme dangers that the crew and passengers faced, including the loss of their ship, everyone was able to abandon the dying ship and safely reach the shore.

Paul on Malta (28:1–10)

Paul and the rest of the survivors soon learned that they were on the island of Malta. Originally, Malta had been populated by Phoenicians, but by 218 B.C. it had come under the control of Rome. The author records that the "natives" (NRSV) or "islanders" (NIV) showed these stranded travelers "unusual kindness" (28:2). The Greek for "natives" or "islanders" (*barbaroi*) literally means "foreigners" or "barbarians"—i.e., Gentiles who did not speak Greek. Most native Maltese spoke Punic, a Semitic language. Also, while most travelers might have expected hostility from the native population, these non-Romans showed "unusual kindness" (*philanthropia*) to them, i.e., hospitality.

This portion of the story began with Paul, who had appealed to Caesar and been put on ship to be taken to Rome. The apostle's survival of the horrific storm and shipwreck was a demonstration for the writer that no obstacle, whether natural or demonic, would prevent Paul from accomplishing God's will for him in Rome. This theme is continued in the story of Paul and the snake. Luke sets the context of the story by stating that it was cold and had begun to rain. Thus, to keep themselves warm and to dry their clothes, someone started a camp fire. In the process of gathering wood for the fire, Paul was bitten by a snake. There was an ancient Greek poem that told of a murderer who escaped in a storm at sea and was eventually shipwrecked on the Libyan coast only to be killed by a snake. The point of the poem is that one cannot run away from justice. Perhaps this or some other similar legend may have been behind the natives' conclusion that Paul had been bitten because he was a murderer who had not been able to escape from justice due him. However, Paul simply shook the snake off of him into the fire and suffered no ill effects from the snakebite. Paul's survival of the snakebite was a demonstration of his righteousness and God's presence with him. Some even considered him to be a god. For Luke, Paul's deliverance from the snake, like his deliverance from the storm and shipwreck, testified to God's protection of Paul so that he might be able to testify of Jesus in Rome.

Paul's Ministry on Malta

Luke's story shifts from the group's survival on the island to Paul's encounter with and ministry to the residents of Malta. The leading man of the island was called Publius. He not only was very wealthy but also was likely a Rome-appointed official. Publius is described by Acts as very welcoming and hospitable to Paul and the others. The narrative continues by noting that Publius' father was very ill with a fever and dysentery. The text states that Paul went into the place where the sick father was, laid his hands on the man, and prayed. The story of the healing of Publius' father recalls the healing miracles of Jesus in the Gospels and also parallels Peter's healing of Aeneas and Dorcas (9:32–42). When news spread that Paul had healed the father of Publius, Luke says that the rest on the island who were sick came to Paul and were healed. In grateful response to Paul's healing ministry, the islanders honored Paul and those with him and furnished them with all necessary supplies as they prepared to set sail for Rome on a different ship. Luke does not record any sermon or even abbreviated message by Paul while on Malta. In fact, Luke records no words of Paul during his stay on the island. Furthermore, Luke gives no record of conversions on Malta. One might conclude that Publius and others who were healed came to faith in Jesus, but there is no mention of it. What Luke describes is Paul providing for the people's need regardless of their faith.

From Malta to Rome (28:11–15)

After spending three months on Malta waiting for the end of winter, Paul and company boarded another Alexandrian ship. Luke notes that this ship had the "Twin Brothers" (Greek, *Dioscuri*) figurehead. Usually *Dioscuri* refers to the twin sons of Zeus, Castor (*Kastor*) and Pollux (*Polydeuke*). These two were venerated as astral deities by many ancient sailors, who saw their constellations in the night sky. The first stop for this ship was Syracuse, the Roman capital of the province of Sicily. Syracuse was originally an ancient Greek colony and was the site of a key battle in the war between Athens and Sparta. They stayed in Syracuse for three days and then went on to Rhegium, an ancient Port city located on the tip of the boot of Italy. After a one-day stay there, the ship moved on to Puteoli, a commercial harbor town on the west coast of Italy. All of Rome's imports of grain from Egypt passed through this town. Puteoli also was the chief port of entry for people coming from Sicily. Luke says Paul found fellow believers in the town and was allowed to stay with them for seven days. They left Puteoli and traveled northward to Rome. Most likely, the rest of journey to Rome from Puteoli was on land. As Paul made his way there, Luke mentions believers from the Forum of Appius (forty-three miles from Rome) and Three Taverns (thirty-three miles from Rome) came out to meet and encourage Paul.

Paul in Rome (28:16–31)

After Paul arrived in Rome, he was put under house arrest and guarded by a soldier. The unusually favorable treatment Paul received while a prisoner may have been the result of a favorable report by Festus, who sent him to Rome, or because Paul was regarded as a very important person.

Paul's Testimony to Jews in Rome

Three days after he arrived in Rome, Paul took the initiative and reached out to leaders of the Jewish community. Since Paul had originally been arrested and charged with a crime by the Jerusalem temple leadership, Paul decided to make it clear to these leaders that he was innocent of the charges against him. He particularly stressed that he had not acted in any way that could be interpreted as hostile or in opposition to the people of Israel or their traditions. Paul briefly reviewed his arrest and trial, noting that he was arrested in Jerusalem and handed over to the Romans, who initially determined that he was not guilty of any capital crime and should be released. Nevertheless, when the Jewish leaders strenuously objected to the idea of Paul's release, he appealed to the emperor. Rather than being guilty of rejecting the faith of Abraham, Isaac, and Jacob or the Law that was given through Moses, Paul claimed that he was in fact on trial because of the hope of Israel: a hope in the coming of the Messiah, the restoration of the kingdom, and the resurrection of the dead. Paul contended he had not left his childhood faith but rather found in Messiah Jesus its ultimate fulfillment.

The Jewish leaders responded that they were completely unfamiliar with the controversies surrounding him. Yet, while they did not have an opinion about Paul, they apparently had one concerning the Jesus movement. At least, they were aware that within most Jewish communities Christianity was generally looked down upon. It should be noted that there apparently had been some kind of conflict in Rome between messianic and non-messianic Jews prior to Paul's arrival. The Roman historian Suetonius speaks of a disturbance in the Jewish quarter surrounding, or instigated by, a certain Chrestus (most likely a misspelling of *Christos*, or Christ), which led to Emperor Claudius expelling from Rome all Jews, both believers in Jesus and non-believers (*Claudius* 25.4). Nevertheless, the leaders were willing to keep an open mind and allow Paul to explain the beliefs of this messianic movement.

At Paul's second meeting with the Jews, Luke notes that a large number of Jews came to hear Paul. Acts summarizes Paul's message as a testimony about the kingdom of God and about Jesus from the Law and Prophets. It may be that Paul's message about the kingdom rejected political and exclusively Jewish institutions. For Paul, the kingdom of God is the reign of God in the heart of anyone who has faith in Jesus, whether Jew or Gentile. As for Jesus, Paul most likely sought to show that the Law and Prophets testified that Jesus was the long awaited Messiah and that it was necessary for him to die and be raised from the dead. Luke states that "some" (28:24) were convinced, which is a way of saying most were unconvinced. Paul had not been successful in converting this Jewish audience. Aware that his audience had mostly rejected his message, Paul quoted from Isaiah 6:26–27, suggesting that most Jews have and would reject the gospel. Paul may have seen himself in the role of a prophet like Isaiah. As Isaiah prophesied to sinful humanity, especially Israel, so Paul did as well. Furthermore, while the rejection of the gospel by these Jewish leaders was tragic, it could also be seen as an opportunity to bring the good news to the Gentiles.

Luke concludes his story by stating that Paul preached for two years about the kingdom of God and Jesus Christ "with all boldness and without hindrance" (28:31). So, while Paul was in prison and his fate was yet to be resolved, there is a note of triumph. This triumph was due to the fact that Paul had brought the gospel to Rome. In so doing, he fulfilled the mission God had given to him at his conversion. Moreover, when Paul came and testified in Rome, he fulfilled the greater mission Jesus had given the church at the beginning of Acts. Nevertheless, even though this part of God's mission to the world had been accomplished, the story is still not over. The mission is not really complete. Wherever there are new territories and places for the gospel to reach and new peoples to transform, the story of Acts continues. And because the real actor in Acts is God through the Holy Spirit, the community of Jesus can be assured that that proclamation will go forth with boldness, without undue hindrance, and ultimately in victory.

For Further Study

Important Names and Terms

- Julius
- The Fast
- Myra
- Fair Havens
- Northeaster
- The Syrtis
- Malta
- Publius
- Castor
- Puteoli

Questions

1. Review the occasions during the voyage when Paul acted as if he were in charge.
2. What does the voyage and shipwreck of Paul tell the reader about the nature of God and his work?
3. Looking at the entire Book of Acts, what is its primary message or theme?

Selected Bibliography

Ash, Anthony Lee. *The Acts of the Apostles*. Vol. 1: *1:1—12:25*. Living Word Commentary 6. Austin, TX: Sweet Publishing, 1979.

Blaiklock, E. M. *The Acts of the Apostles: An Historical Commentary*. Tyndale New Testament Commentaries. Grand Rapids: Eerdmans, 1959.

Bruce, F. F. *The Book of Acts*. New International Commentary on the New Testament. Grand Rapids: Eerdmans, 1988.

Martin, Ralph, and Peter H. Davids, editors. *Dictionary of the Later New Testament and Its Developments*. Downers Grove, IL: InterVarsity, 1997.

Ferguson, Everett. *Backgrounds of Early Christianity*. Grand Rapids: Eerdmans, 1987.

Fitzmyer, Joseph A. *The Acts of the Apostles*. New York: Doubleday, 1998.

Grant, Michael. *History of Rome*. New York: Scribner's, 1978.

Jervell, Jacob. *The Theology of the Acts of the Apostles*. New Testament Theology. Cambridge: Cambridge University Press, 1996.

Johnson, Luke Timothy. *The Acts of the Apostles*. Sacra pagina 5. Collegeville, MN: Liturgical, 1992.

Kee, Howard Clark. *Good News to the Ends of the Earth: The Theology of Acts*. London: SCM, 1990.

Marshall, I. Howard. *The Acts of the Apostles: An Introduction and Commentary*. Tyndale New Testament Commentaries. Grand Rapids: Eerdmans, 1980.

Marshall, I. Howard. *Luke: Historian and Theologian*. 2nd ed. Downers Grove, IL: InterVarsity, 1979.

Oster, Richard. *The Acts of the Apostles*. Vol. 2: *13:1—28:31*. Living Word Commentary 6. Austin, TX: Sweet Publishing, 1979.

Neil, William. *The Acts of the Apostles*. New Century Bible Commentary 44. Grand Rapids: Eerdmans, 1981.

Powell, Mark Allen. *What Are They Saying About Acts?* New York: Paulist, 1991.

Whitson, William, translator. *The New Complete Works of Josephus*. Rev. ed. Grand Rapids: Kregel, 1999.

Williams, David John. *Acts*. New International Biblical Commentary 5. Peabody, MA: Hendrickson, 1990.

Willimon, William H. *Acts*. Interpretation. Atlanta: John Knox, 1988.

Wise, Michael, Martin Abegg, Jr., and Edward Cook, translators. *The Dead Sea Scroll: A New Translation*. New York: Harper Collins Publishers, 1999.

Witherington, Ben, III. *The Acts of the Apostles: A Socio-Rhetorical Commentary*. Grand Rapids: Eerdmans, 1998.

www.ingramcontent.com/pod-product-compliance
Lightning Source LLC
Chambersburg PA
CBHW071453150426
43191CB00008B/1333